Remembering My Home

A TRIBUTE TO MY PARENTS

Remembering My Home

A TRIBUTE TO MY PARENTS

Norman I. Sison

ABOOKS

Alive Book Publishing

Additional copies may be ordered from the publisher for
educational, business, promotional or premium use.
For information, contact ALIVE Book Publishing at:
alivebookpublishing.com

Book Interior and Cover Design by Alex P. Johnson

ISBN 13
978-1-63132-179-5

Library of Congress Control Number: 2022917758
Library of Congress Cataloging-in-Publication Data
is available upon request.

First Edition

Published in the United States of America by ALIVE Book Publishing
an imprint of Advanced Publishing LLC, Alamo, California, USA
alivebookpublishing.com

PRINTED IN THE UNITED STATES OF AMERICA

10 9 8 7 6 5 4 3 2 1

I dedicate this book to my parents,

Jose and Fe Sison.

Thank you for the journey with you.

ACKNOWLEDGMENTS

My gratitude to my publishers, Eric and Peggy Johnson, of Alive Book Publishing for believing in me. You were astonishing with your insight and considerations to revisions that I made in the manuscript and other requests during the process of publication. I deeply appreciate your professional advice and all-out support in the publication of this book. Thank you for putting it all together.

Thank you to my editor Lily O'brien, for your commitment in editing my book. You did an amazing job. You are a precious jewel. Thank you to Alex Johnson, Art Director of Alive Book Publishing, for designing a wonderful cover for my book. Your talent and creative eye made the cover design just the way I wanted it. You are a true artist.

A special thank you to Millicent Lenore McCormack, for encouraging me to write and be good at it. Your words of inspiration and support guided my steps to get back into writing. Thank you to my sister Marissa, for your unwavering moral support, patience and understanding. My sister lent me her new and updated computer for me to use for the whole time I wrote my book. Since I was not proficient in computer, she was always there to assist me.

Thank you to Nubie, Ivan Luke, Pola and Maximus Kjell, for serving as my love and inspiration. May you keep and cherish our family memories in your hearts. Thank you to my Dad and Mom, for leaving me wonderful memories to write about and share.

Lastly, thank you dear God, Mother Mary, Papa Joseph and Jesus, for being instrumental in making this writing project possible. This book could not have been put together without your guidance and blessing. I will treasure this gift for the rest of my life.

CONTENTS

PROLOGUE

I wrote this narrative to pay tribute to my parents, and at the same time, to all parents. It was inspired by the memories I had through the years when I lived with them in the United States. When my parents passed away, I missed them so much. Reminiscing about them brought back vivid memories of both happy and sad moments.

At first, I thought those memories about my parents were just ordinary moments of recollecting and forgetting. But as I look back and reflect, those memories endured and served as my link to the past. They preserved the bygone years and gave life to moments that we spent together. In time, I came to cherish the treasure trove of memories about my parents, and particularly, those about the significant parts of our lives that we spent together that taught me lessons and helped mold my character.

There were many things that reminded me of my parents, like their favorite foods, restaurants, Christmas, New Year's, their traits and words of advice, Mom's perfume and her cooking, and Dad's big voice and humor. My recollection of my parents and my life with them in the U.S. is voluminous. I used to internalize those memories and live with them every day. I thought that if I had the opportunity to piece the collection of those memories into one long story, it could have the potential to inspire other people, especially the younger generation, to better understand their parents and enhance their relationships with them. That notion led me to embark on a small writing project that evolved into this narrative.

Writing this narrative became a part of my healing process from the grief brought about by my parents' passing. It also led me to various discoveries and realizations about the true essence of family and parental love. With this narrative, I would like to honor the memory of my father and mother. And because the setting is in the U.S., it also carries an undertone of the Filipino immigrant story in America.

This narrative is a work of fiction, but it was inspired by true events culled from my recollections about my parents and stories from other people. Most of the names, dates, and places in the story are fictional. Any resemblance of the characters to actual persons, living or dead, is coincidental.

It was my intention to present a story that all people can relate to and learn from in so far as their relationships with their parents and family are concerned. In one way or another, we all experience love, happiness, sadness, challenges, struggles, bonding, misunderstandings, and understandings with our parents and family. May this book present insights about family life that would help strengthen family relationships and inspire readers to keep family values.

May this book inspire the reader to value the important role of parents in our lives. May we always remember their love and sacrifices. May we continue to love and respect them in return, whether they are still living or have passed away. May this small tribute to my parents inspire others to give tribute to their own parents and encourage them to cherish fond memories of them as well.

As we learn to love and respect our parents with more depth and insight, we also need to realize what a big part of our lives they are or were. As you read this simple narrative, it is my hope that it will bring you realizations and discoveries about your own parents, as well as yourself. May you always keep your memories about them in your hearts.

It is an honor to be able to pay tribute to my parents in any possible way that I can, even though they have passed on. It is a privilege to be able to honor them by writing a book about them and wholeheartedly dedicating it to them.

CHAPTER ONE
VISIT

My name is Frank. The first time I visited my parents in the United States was in 2001 with my wife Trina and our son Ken. Ever since my parents had migrated to the US in 1995, they had been back to the Philippines only once in 2001 on a Balikbayan trip, a special tourism program for Filipinos who were overseas designed to encourage them to go back and visit the Philippines. When my family and I came to the U.S., they were emotional and exhilarated. They had been homesick and missed the whole family so much.

During our first visit, Trina, Ken, who was five years old at that time, and I went to Disneyland, Universal Studios, Golden Gate Park, Fisherman's Wharf, Pier 39, Napa Valley, Las Vegas, and many other places. We visited family and friends. We shared so much fun and excitement together. After a month, Trina and Ken returned to the Philippines but I extended my stay in the US for two more months to bond with my parents.

The second time I visited my parents in the United States was in March 2003 on a bright California day. The day I arrived, the San Francisco International Airport was crowded with passengers. Waiting time at the passenger processing area was protracted because the queue was slow to budge. Tighter security measures were being enforced in the aftermath of the 9/11 tragedy.

When it was my turn to process my entry, the Customs and Border Protection Officer instructed me to proceed to the secondary screening room. When I heard that, I uncomfortably smelled trouble. It shook the jetlag out of me.

"What the hell did I get myself into?

"Do I look like a terrorist?"

"Am I carrying contraband?"

"Am I going to be sent back to the Philippines?"

I was not being paranoid, but I did ask myself those questions as I walked toward the secondary screening room. If I had to answer those questions one by one, I was confident that none of them would be a problem. I knew I would probably just be asked some questions and be released in one piece. I was relaxed until I entered the designated office. I saw an officer at the front desk yelling at one of the passengers, an elderly Asian woman.

"I told you to sit down!" he shouted angrily at her as she fidgeted and then returned to her seat.

After seeing that, I presumed I was wandering into hostile territory. At least I knew what I am up against.

In a short while, my name was called. The officer assigned to me turned out to be cordial but tough on his questions. I knew the officer was just doing his job as his questions were standard operations procedure. He tried to squeeze information out of me about the last time I had been in the U.S. He tried to trap me into admitting that I had worked in the U.S. when I came in 2001. I had stayed for more than three months during my first U.S. visit but never looked for employment. I spent all of that time bonding with my parents.

I told the officer that I was telling him the truth and had

nothing to hide. To convince him, I brought out whatever documents I had for him to peruse. Since the officer was holding my current passport, I brought out all my old passports, my company ID, membership and organization IDs, my Philippine driver's license, and even my credit cards for him to check. I wrote down a list of numbers that he could call in the U.S. and the Philippines to verify my identity and record.

My cooperation, honesty and openness helped to speed up and facilitate my release. My reinspection had gone like a walk in the park. As I left the room, I noticed the old lady was not sitting in the reception area anymore. From what the people there told me, she had been released too. I was doubly happy for her.

From the airport terminal, I took the BART (Bay Area Rapid Transit) going to Concord in the East Bay. While on the train, I called my father, who quickly picked up the phone.

"Hello, *anak* (my child). Are you at the airport now?" he eagerly asked. My parents were expecting my call. It was meant to inform them that I had arrived. We had pre-planned our meeting arrangement in Concord.

"Daddy, I'm on BART. See you later."

I dialed Mom's phone next. As soon as she said hello, I blurted out excitedly, "Mommy, I'm here. Will see you later."

My parents could not wait to see me. I wondered what would have happened if I had been declared inadmissible. What would I be telling them? That I was waiting for the next available flight back to the Philippines? I could only imagine what my parents' reaction would have been—quite a killjoy to their excitement.

From the Concord BART Station I walked down four blocks on Grant Street to go downtown. With my backpack on my back, I rolled my carry-on bag on top of my spinner suitcase on the sidewalk. In my left hand, I carried a medium-sized plastic bag containing a small replica of Our Lady of Manaoag, the Patron Saint of the Province of Pangasinan.

Upon reaching Willow Pass Road, I decided I wanted to get something at Starbucks which was just a few steps away. I ordered a warmed-up ham and cheese croissant and a large Mocha Frappuccino to go. As soon as I got my order, I walked toward Todos Santos Plaza which was across the street. I had to wait for my parents who were still at work. It was 2:30 p.m. and Dad was not coming home until 4:30 p.m. I had a lot of time to kill. As soon as I found a bench to sit on, I shoveled down my ham and cheese croissant for my late lunch.

I had come full circle in this tree-lined square plaza where my parents and I had strolled, exercised, and picnicked on the park tables. At the plaza, we had bought organic fruits and vegetables, and other goodies during the Farmers' Market every Tuesday, and in the summer, every Tuesday and Thursday. At the plaza, we had watched scheduled shows and concerts. At night, the whole plaza glittered with holiday lights year-round. From the plaza, my parents' apartment was just a stone's throw away, in one of those rows of apartments on Colfax Street.

At past 4 p.m., I headed to my parents' apartment and waited on the porch. Dad arrived after just a few minutes. He embraced me tightly to welcome me. As soon as I was inside the apartment, I put my luggage aside in one corner of the living room and placed the small statue of Mother

Mary on the bedroom altar. Dad sat at the dining table and chomped on a burger, our *merienda* (snack) that he had bought on his way home. Since I had eaten a late lunch, I put my burger in the refrigerator and sat down on the sofa to watch TV. Before 7 p.m., we went to pick up Mom at K-Mart on Clayton Road.

My parents, Juancho and Maria, came to the U.S. as retirees from the Philippines. Dad was a railway officer and had a thriving business on the side. Mom was the dean of the college of nursing at a local university based in Pangasinan, a province north of Manila.

Mom had a petition from her sister while Dad had a petition from his brother. Relative petitions took time to process. Mom's petition from her sister, *Tita* (the Filipino term for auntie) Paz came up first to be processed. It took all of eighteen years before my parents were able to come to the U.S. By the time they arrived, they were already in their mid-sixties.

While they were waiting for their petitions, Mom was looking forward to reuniting with her mother, who had been living with *Tita* Paz's family in the U.S. for quite a long time. Mom's mother and *Tita* Paz were hoping that Mom could come sooner because they missed each other so much. Sadly, my grandmother passed away a few years before Dad and Mom were able to come to the U.S. When my parents finally did move in the U.S., they would often visit my grandmother's niche at the cemetery located about six miles from *Tita* Paz's house.

My parents had first lived with *Tita* Paz in Walnut Creek, California, a city next to Concord, before they settled down on their own. *Tita* Paz and her family had been long-time residents in the U.S. My aunt was a U.S. scholar who earned her master's degree in the U.S., and then worked as a speech therapist/teacher at the Contra Costa County Office of Education. When Dad did not have a car yet, she was the one who patiently drove my parents to job interviews. Later, when my parents were already employed, she drove them to their workplaces as well. *Tita* Paz, the youngest of Mom's siblings, had the time to drive my parents because she had recently retired from her job.

When Dad and I picked up Mom at work, she embraced me as she shed tears of happiness to see me again. In the apartment, we called family members in the Philippines, one after the other, to tell them I had arrived safely and was now at home with Dad and Mom. We called Trina and Ken, and our youngest sister, Chloe, who was then in high school and lived with *Kuya* (the Filipino term for older brother) Steve. We then called *Kuya* Steve and *Kuya* James.

We had another sister, *Ate* (the Filipino term for older sister) Julia, who was the second oldest among my siblings. She died from Leukemia when she was just two years old, on her birthday. During that time, treatment and medication for Leukemia was not as advanced and high tech. My parents were fond of her. They would always remember her and tell us stories about her. They told us that *Ate* Julia as a toddler had already demonstrated her talent for singing and dancing.

It was only our oldest brother, *Kuya* Steve, who got to be with *Ate* Julia. She died many years before the rest of us among her siblings were born. Mom had put together an album, complete with a tearjerking narrative and montage of captioned photos in honor of my sister's memory. The album and the stories my parents affectionately shared with us endeared us to her. Because of my sister's disease, I became aware of Leukemia awareness programs, fundraising events for Leukemia research and medical missions. I would sometimes donate a few dollars to Leukemia organizations in honor of my sister's memory.

Whenever we called the family in the Philippines, we talked to everyone like we were going around in circle. Dad, Mom, and I would talk to my brothers. After that, my brothers would pass the phone to my sisters-in-law. Then my sisters-in-law would pass the phone to my nephews and nieces, and then the phone would go back to my brothers for winding up. The three of us in the U.S. would also pass the phone back and forth to each other so we could talk to everyone. Too bad we did not have group chats or video-conferences yet at that time. It would have been the perfect platform for us to have a virtual, interactive family communication streaming live from different locations.

After our calls, my parents and I sat down to do a lot of catching up with each other. As we enjoyed exchanging stories, Mom started to heat up the mouthwatering dishes she had prepared earlier. She cooked Chicken Adobo (chicken cooked in soy sauce and vinegar), Kare-Kare (beef and ox tail stew cooked with vegetables and peanut butter), and Sinigang na Hipon (shrimp in sour soup).

I told Mom in jest, "Mom, I have those dishes all the time in the Philippines. You should have cooked American dishes for me instead."

Mom lovingly responded, "Frank, don't you know that what you've been missing is my cooking? Even if you have those dishes back home all the time, my cooking is different. You're now enjoying Mom's cooking."

Mom was right. I enjoyed the hearty meals that she made. It had been a long time since I had been able to savor her wonderful cooking. Mom's dishes still had those same flavors that we grew up with. It made you feel like you were back home in the Philippines. And good food would pave the way to good conversation. As we ate, we continued catching up with each other with a surplus of smiles, laughter, and delight. As if I could not wait for the next meal, I asked Mom if I could have *Bistek Tagalog* (beef sautéed in soy sauce) and calamansi, a Filipino citrus fruit, the next day. My request showed how much I loved and missed her cooking. My mother, amiable as she was, gave me a positive response.

After dinner, it was time to give the *pasalubong* (gift). I had brought only a few clothes and personal items with me. The rest of my luggage was filled to the brim with *pasalubongs*. The *pasalubongs* consisted of cooked foods like *Egado* (strips of pork tenderloin, pork liver and other entrails like pork kidney, braised in vinegar and soy sauce), *Lechon Paksiw* (chopped leftover lechon aka roast pig cooked with liver sauce or lechon sauce, vinegar and spices), and some other dishes that do not spoil easily. Those were placed in small plastic jars or bottle containers or carefully packed in plastic bags and canned.

We also had *tuyo tunsoy* (dried salted herring), *kaling* (dried belt fish), *burong manga* (pickled mango in salt), *lingayen bagoong* (a condiment made of fermented fish), as well as sweets like *pastillas* (milk-based confection), *bocayo* (coconut candy), and peanut brittle.

Besides food, I also carried *pasalubong* items like native products and shell craft displays, house slippers, including fashion accessories, comfy dusters and Filipiniana dresses (Filipino traditional dresses for women worn on special occasions) for mom, as well as Filipino designed t-shirts and

Barong Tagalogs (Filipino embroidered long-sleeved formal shirts for men) for dad. I also brought letters and photographs from the grandchildren. These *pasalubongs* were given by the whole family to our parents. It was one way of expressing our affection and connecting with them.

The giving of *pasalubongs* is embedded in the Filipino culture. Most of the time, we give things that we know the recipient would need or like to have. When the recipient is the one who comes to visit, he or she would do the same thing—give gifts to family and friends. *Pasalubongs*, whether big or small, expensive or inexpensive, are always appreciated. What always counted was the thought and the preservation of a Filipino custom or tradition that strengthened the bonds within family and friends.

My parents lived in a small one-bedroom apartment they called home. The bedroom and bathroom were separated from a square space where the living room, dining area, and kitchen were positioned next to each other. We slept late as we enjoyed the evening, eating and bonding with each other. I slept on the sofa in the living room. I was tired but thankful for the safe trip, and happy to see my parents again. I said my prayers, thanking the Lord for the blessings and gift of time he had given me to spend with my parents. I snuggled up in my blanket and went into a deep slumber with the sound of serenity that resonated in the cold and darkness of the night.

After a few hours had passed, I was awakened by the light that was switched on in the kitchen. I opened my drowsy eyes slightly to peek at what was going on. I saw Mom, quietly preparing Dad's lunchbox that he would bring to work. Soon, I saw Dad come out of the bedroom dressed up in his work uniform. My father, despite his white hair, was sprightly and burly in his five-foot-seven frame. He sat down with my mother at the dining table to sip coffee while they talked in whispers so they would not disturb my slumber. At 6 a.m., Dad kissed Mom goodbye and left to drive to work. He worked as distribution clerk at the John Muir Health Medical Center in Walnut Creek, one of the best hospitals in Northern California.

At 9 a.m., it was Mom's turn to leave for work. I walked her to the bus stop by the BART station which is five blocks away. I particularly walked closely with her when she crossed the street to make sure she was safe because she walked slowly. I did not want her to get ran over by a careless driver. My mother was five feet tall, a bit chubby, and fair-skinned with strands of white and grey hair. At the bus stop, I sent her off to work. She worked as a retail sales associate at K-Mart, one of the leading department store chains in the U.S. back then. I walked back to the apartment and ate breakfast that she had prepared for me before she left for work. After breakfast, I lazed around in the sofa listening to music or watching TV the whole day. That was my yawny routine after my arrival in Concord.

During those times, I would sometimes come by Peet's to grab a cappuccino after sending Mom off to work at the bus stop. I would be tempted to sit at Todos Santos Plaza for a while to people watch or while away time as a way to break the monotony. I would then head back to the apartment to have breakfast or early lunch. To fight my idleness and boredom, and give my parents something to cheer up about, I came up with a "daily agenda" to follow. I washed dishes, made Dad and Mom's bed, dusted off the furniture and vacuumed the carpet. Besides the regular chores, I would try to perform one major chore a day, like cleaning the toilet, doing the laundry, or whatever major chore I had planned to do for that day.

My parents never complained about my idleness. They never asked me to do all those chores. I volunteered to do them. I took it as a self-imposed obligation. It was the least I could do while vacationing with them. I was happy and felt at home doing the chores. Besides, I had nothing else to do. It was a way to break my dormant and humdrum life. On top of that, I wanted to surprise my parents. Whenever they arrive home from work, they were always tired. When the chores were done, they could take a respite before we gathered at the table for dinner.

It was an easy endeavor. When I am done with the chores, I had nothing else to do but turn on the radio or watch TV. I flipped through the channels from CNN, ESPN, TNT, ABC, NBC, CBS, PBS, Fox, History, Discovery to National Geographic. I watched tabloid talk shows like "The Jerry Springer Show" and "The Maury Show" which were something new to me, a different genre, which became a part of my discovery about the heart and soul of American society. Some people viewed it as a trash. I opened my eyes to it as a presentation of the many facets, realities and by-products in many modern, progressive and liberated environments. I found it funny, entertaining, and informative as it momentarily helped rid the boredom and monotony. I also watched "Judge Judy," "COPS," "NBA," "The Price is Right," "Jeopardy," and other game shows, newscasts, documentaries and features. My parents had not yet subscribed to the Filipino channels at that time. We watched Philippine newscasts on KTSF 26. By 4:30 p.m., Dad would arrive and we would devour the *merienda* that he had bought for that afternoon. Just before 7 p.m., we would pick up Mom at K-Mart.

Weekends were Dad and Mom's days off, although sometimes Mom worked Saturdays. On Saturdays, we shopped for the week's provisions and ate out. We would go to Safeway and Costco where Mom enjoyed the *patikim* (product promotion through free food tasting). At times, when we needed to buy Filipino ingredients and had cravings for Filipino food, we drove farther to Vallejo, which is more than fifteen miles from Concord. There, we shopped at Island Pacific, a Filipino supermarket chain in the US. In Vallejo, there were many Filipino restaurants, including Filipino popular ones like Jollibee and Max's where we can go to eat. At that time, Concord had only one small Filipino grocery on Clayton Road, the Oriental Food Market. The neighboring city of Pleasant Hill had one Asian supermarket but carried a limited variety of Filipino products.

Back then, there was only one Filipino restaurant in Concord that we knew of. If I am recalling it correctly, it was called Aroma and was located on Broadway. When I came in 2003, it had closed down. Sometime later, Goldilocks, a popular Filipino restaurant, opened in Pleasant Hill. Another Filipino restaurant followed suit somewhere on Clayton Road in Concord. After a few years, those restaurants, including the Asian supermarket in Pleasant Hill, closed down.

Eventually around 2009, Seafood City, another Filipino supermarket chain in the U.S. opened, hosting a bevy of popular Filipino fast-food chains like Jollibee, Red Ribbons, Goldilocks, and Chow King. This was followed by the opening of 99 Ranch Market, an Asian supermarket chain in the U.S. that was also popular with Filipinos. Both were located in Concord.

Sundays were lazy days. We woke up late, ate breakfast

late, and listened to music or watched TV the whole day. Late in the afternoon, we would go to Mass at Queen of All Saints Church, just three blocks from our apartment, and then have dinner out afterwards. Our family indulged in food because we love to eat and enjoy trying out various restaurants. If we had time, we would watch a movie at Brenden Theaters in downtown Concord or at Century 14 in downtown Walnut Creek.

CHAPTER 2
THE ACCIDENT

One Sunday afternoon after attending Mass, we got caught in a car accident. The accident overturned the course of my direction in life. It accidentally flipped over my plans in life. Some people say there are really no accidents in life. They believed that accidents that happen are planned or destined to happen. There are reasons behind why things happen to us, whether they are good things or bad things. We would just realize those reasons as we live and go through life's vicissitudes.

That Sunday, we were leisurely traversing Concord Avenue in Dad's blue Volvo 240 DL sedan, a car given to him by his doctor-niece. Dad was behind the wheel. I was sitting in the front passenger seat while Mom was comfortably sitting in the back. We were on our way to dinner at a Chinese restaurant in Pleasant Hill. The three of us were starving. We were vivaciously talking about what we were going to order. Dad told us he would like to order his favorite Hong Kong Pan Fried Noodles Combo and Salt and Pepper Pork. Mom was craving for the Honey Walnut Prawns and Egg Foo Young. I was planning to order my favorite BBQ Pork Fried Rice and the Sizzling Beef Platter.

As we hit the intersection between Commerce Avenue and Highway 242, a red car coming from Commerce Avenue ran the red light. At that very moment, a truck was proceeding to pass from the opposite direction of Concord Avenue. The red car could have stopped while it still had time to avoid a crash. Instead, it sped up so it could pass the intersection ahead of the truck to avoid hitting it. The red car driver executed a feat by not hitting the truck, albeit by a slim margin, but unfortunately, the red car careered across the street and ended up ramming smack into the side of our car. We were T-boned, and the impact pushed our car onto the curb on our right. Dad had the presence of mind to maneuver his car to avoid crashing into other cars passing on the road. We ran aground next to the sidewalk from the middle lane of the street.

We did not see it coming. Dad, Mom, and I were left stunned for a moment. We were wondering what had happened. When I came to my senses, I immediately checked Mom and Dad for any injuries. At that time, what was visible to me were only minor bruises on their arms. I would find out later that most of our injuries were concentrated on our legs which I did not see because we were all wearing pants. At that time, I was just greatly relieved that my parents were not bloodied or mangled.

I rushed to the other car that hit us to check if anybody was hurt. Dad followed behind me closely. The other car had ended up grounded right in the middle of the intersection. The car's body was mostly intact, but the front was wrecked, and the hood had opened up with a conspicuous bent. On the pavement around the car, I saw small fragments of car parts scattered, detached, and thrown aimlessly around, resulting from the impact of the crash.

The driver of the car that hit us was a woman who looked like she was in her forties, along with what I presumed were her two elementary-school-age daughters. The three of them remained seated in their car looking unhurt, but crying. They were most likely shaken. To calm them down I told them, "Hang in there. Everything's going to be alright. Help is coming soon."

They stared at me and just continued crying. Dad and I walked back to our car where Mom remained seated inside. Not long after, I heard emergency sirens coming our way. An ambulance transported my parents and me to the John Muir Health, Concord Medical Center.

At the hospital, we were informed about the extent of our injuries. We did not suffer life-threatening injuries but as we knew it, we had been injured. Dad sustained small cracks on two of his left ribs (his side of the car took the brunt of the crash), and contusions on his legs and arms. Mom had acquired multiple contusions on her legs and a few on her arms. Mine were minor contusions on my legs. We were discharged with instructions to come back for a checkup.

The next day, Dad and Mom's legs turned black and blue. They felt pain in their legs, arms, neck and back. They experienced pain walking. They were not able to work for two weeks. Their aging bodies were more susceptible to injuries from the impact of the crash. We underwent chiropractic treatment for some time.

Meanwhile, since I was the least injured, I temporarily took over the reign of cooking, cleaning, washing dishes and running errands while Dad and Mom recuperated. My parents did not have to ask me to do that. It was the only way I could be of help to them. Besides, I had been volunteering to do that since I arrived.

When the three of us would talk about the accident, we would mention the solid, hard and well-built body of the Volvo. The car model was an 80's or 90's Volvo. We agreed that it could have been one of the factors that saved us from further injuries. It might have been different if we had been driving a car more compact and less sturdy. It was the driver's side of our car that was heavily damaged. If we had it fixed, it would cost so much that it was better to buy a new car. We were sad to let go of it. We loved that car. Dad had a sentimental value for it because it was his first car in the U.S. We replaced it with a brand-new car, the latest model of the Honda Pilot SUV.

When Dad was able to walk better, we went to the Concord Police Station to get a copy of the police report about the accident. What we read from the statement of the other driver demoralized us. She reported that we were the ones who hit her car. It was a good thing that her statement was invalidated by the statements given by three voluntary witnesses. The three witnesses stated we were not at fault, and that it was the other car who had hit us after beating the red light.

We did not have any prior knowledge about nor had asked the three witnesses to give statements to the police. We never even met or saw them. They happened to be driving in that area at the time of the accident and saw what happened. They had pulled over to see what help they could possibly extend to anyone in need. We only got to know about their involvement after reading the police report. We regretted not being able to personally meet and thank them for their help and concern. They had helped us without asking for recognition or reward. We were very thankful to have sampled the power of the American spirit and good values that had benefitted us during that time when we were in distress and in dire need of help.

The accident got me into some reflection. "Who would

help my parents if something like this happened when I wasn't here?" I was set to fly back to the Philippines in three weeks. "Should I extend my stay or stay for good?" In hindsight, my parents could stand on their own. They were not asking me to stay to help them. We have family and friends who were more than willing to help but, of course, they could not be there all the time. When the accident happened, I saw how important it was that there was somebody in the family by their side who could help them in any way and at any time. I wanted to make a difference in my aging parents' lives. I could not bear to leave them on their own.

"What if they got sick?"

"Who's going to take care of them?"

On the other hand, my family in the Philippines was waiting for me to come back home. I was in a quandary. I was caught between my family in the U.S., vis-à-vis my parents, and my family back home. They were of the same level of importance to me. It was like if I chose one, I would feel guilty for the other. Trina and I seriously weighed in on the matter. We considered who needed more help at that time, which was my parents. We delved into the ramifications if I chose to stay. That included the need to find work to be able to support my family so I would not be a financial burden on my parents. I would also need to legalize my resident status by looking for a job sponsor.

My colloquy with Trina resurrected my desire to bring my wife and son to the U.S. to give them a better life than what we had in the Philippines. I could not think of a better time to do that than right at that time. Since I was already physically present in the U.S., I thought I should grab the opportunity to start in the place where I already was to pursue my dream. All I needed to do was to take the first step.

The road would be paved for me if it was meant to be.

Eventually, I made up my mind to stay in the U.S. My decision was influenced by my aspirations for my family and my intention to look after my aging parents. My decision was like punching at the moon, but my game plan was to find an employer who was willing to give me work and employment sponsorship at the same time. That was the only way I knew to keep my status legal. I wanted to try my luck and make it on my own. With my wife's support, I filed my resignation from my job as a broadcaster in the Philippines.

Immediately, I kicked off my quest for what many people call the American Dream. Or I would call it my pursuit of a typical Filipino dream. Or simply my personal dream. I was at the threshold of a new journey. Whatever that dream is called, I adamantly took off on my journey and trekked on the road toward that dream.

My parents gave their all-out support to my efforts to find an employer who would sponsor my work visa. They did not want me to stay illegally in the U.S. because they did not want me to suffer the consequences. My mother had filed a family petition for me and my siblings in February, just a month ahead of my arrival in the U.S. which was in March of that same year. The petition would take many years of waiting before I could get a green card. I certainly could not wait that long to start a life in the U.S. I had my B-1/B-2 tourist visa, but it was not an authorization to obtain employment. I was in my twenties and holding a journalism degree, but it did not mean anything at all if I did not possess the legal papers.

The circumstances were not very encouraging as my fields of interest were not even within the list of in-demand jobs in the U.S. Against the odds, I needed to look for a job and an employment sponsor to get a work visa. Looking for a job in my situation was easier said than done. I wondered how much more looking I must do to find a job sponsor. My prospects were slim. I was punching for the moon. I had nothing but hope and courage. I was facing a gamut of obstacles and unfavorable conditions, I had to push myself to take a firm step forward, to start somewhere, anywhere. I had to take a firm stand with my decision. I had to move forward. I could not afford to turn back.

I had always been independent, strong-willed and bullish. I had always wanted to strike out on my own. I never wanted to disturb or depend on anybody else, even on my parents. Now that one factor that made me decide to stay in the U.S. was my parents, I think it was a blessing that I have them to back me up. I would happily take care of and live with them as I pursue my dreams for my family.

I started rolling up my sleeves. My parents did not have computer yet so I relied on the phone, dialing establishments to inquire for openings. Dad and Mom gave me a telephone directory to find business establishments I could call. They supplied me with Filipino and American newspapers so I could check employment ads. My phone inquiries did not yield the desired results, so I decided to take the search outdoors. I took myself out of my comfort zone and went door-to-door, inquiring and applying in person, establishment by establishment.

I started in Concord and scoured multiple cities, especially those accessible by BART. Because I did not have a driver's license or a car, I walked all day, trudging under the heat of the sun. And because I was saving my pocket money, I skipped lunch and bore the pangs of hunger. I knocked on every door, whether they were hiring or not, and turned every city upside down. Those experiences galvanized my determination to find the way to my dream.

America was still reeling from the impact of the 911 tragedy. In March 2003, the administration of President George W. Bush launched the war against Iraq. The US-led war was not only a war against Iraq but a war against terrorism. Some employers had become wary of foreigners, especially those coming from countries with antagonistic stance against the U.S. Having legal papers or appropriate identification was crucial. Many companies were strict on the applicant's identification and status. There was one tactless employer who scoffed at me because of my status in the presence of his employees.

Even if I could not show any documents, there were a few establishments who initially accepted me for employment. I never got the chance to work with any of them though. Those same establishments would later change their minds about hiring me. They realized they could not take the risk of hiring somebody with no legal eligibility to work. Those experiences left me with angst every time.

All along, I knew that I was just taking chances. All my efforts had been going to waste. The irresistible temptation to give up kept slapping me on the face. Sometimes it looked like that was the way to go. I got despondent at times but I trusted that I would make it. Heedless of the uninviting atmosphere, I remained stubborn. I never gave in to the temptation to give up.

Of all the doors I knocked on, the only door that welcomed me with a heart and open arms was the door at home. At the end of the day, I knew that when I entered that door, I would have a sanctuary to stay in. As soon as I made mano (a Filipino gesture of respect to the elderly by bowing and pressing your forehead on their hands) to my parents, I would start feeling the solace of home. Mom would serve our hot dinner and my parents would ask how my day went. I would tell them about my frustrations. They would advise me to be more patient and hope for the best.

To relieve my angst, Dad would share some lighthearted stories about his own experiences when he was applying for a job. He told me a story about the time he was asking for an application form from an office staff member. The staff member's name tag said "Peggy." With Dad's vernacular accent, he greeted her with, "Hello Miss Piggy." The lady sneered back at him. When Dad got the form, he said, "Thank you Miss Piggy." Then she turned her back on Dad.

While he was filling out the application form, Dad asked Mom why the lady was acting that way. Mom asked Dad what he had said to her, and he told her he had greeted her by saying, "Hello Miss Piggy." When the lady passed by them, Mom saw her name tag. It gave her an inkling of what happened. Mom quickly said, "Daddy, the lady's name is Peggy, with an e, not Piggy." Unfortunately, of all the coincidences that can happen in life, the lady was quite extra in her weight. Dad's gaffe was, of course, unintentional. There was no pun intended. He wanted to apologize but feared that his intentions might be misinterpreted. He also worried that it might embarrass the lady more than please her. He decided to just leave it the way it was and keep mum about the incident.

There was another story Dad told me about when he applied for a job as a security officer. Dad wanted that job because he felt he was cut out for it. He had gotten some police training, including how to use a gun, in the Philippines.

He was elated when the interviewer told him that he was being considered for the position. He was asked to come back to submit some documents together with the application form. Then Mom and *Tita* Paz, who were both senior citizens, came into the reception area to pick Dad up. Dad introduced them to the interviewer. The interviewer asked Dad, "How do you plan to get to work?" Dad replied, "My sister-in-law will drive for me." The interviewer reluctantly asked for the application form back, and politely told Dad, "Come back when you're driving," and all of Dad's enthusiasm crumbled away.

One day, Dad and Mom asked me, "How do you deal with your frustrations?" Before I could even reply, they asked me, "What have you learned from it?" They seemed anxious to know my coping mechanism for the challenges that I encountered every day. I told them that I had learned to be tough and thick-skinned. I had learned to put aside my timidity and shyness and be more aggressive and go-getter. I had learned to put aside sentiments and disparage frustrations. I also tried to be street-smart to protect myself from being outsmarted. I boasted to my parents that with my capabilities, I could do a better job than many of the employees I saw working in several establishments.

My response did not sound inspiring to my parents. In a manner typical of Mom, she reminded me to be humble and kind. She added that God favored the humble and kind. She emphasized that if I could practice those virtues, I would be able to master inner strength, forbearance, and self-confidence, and I would develop a better understanding and outlook on life. Dad told me it was all part of the game. He advised me to take things with more patience and wisdom because applying for a job takes time and effort. He told me not to give up.

Before retiring to bed, I called Trina and Ken. I told them engrossing and funny stories from my experiences while looking for a job. I never told them about my disappointments to spare them from worrying. As the night wore on, I thought about my parents' words, which gave me comfort and support. Their words served as food for thought that bolstered my motivation and dynamics in life. They were sufficient to get me inspired for my next day's job search.

To stave off hunger a little longer during the day, I always ate a heavy breakfast. Discreetly, I would take three packets of Skyflakes crackers from the kitchen cupboard and throw them into my backpack. Then I would fill up my water bottle with cold water or juice to wash down the crackers when I would eat them for lunch. I did not realize Mom was cognizant about this. Earlier that morning she had prepared a lunchbox and handed it to me. I carefully put it in my backpack and told her I appreciated it. As I was just about to leave, she fished a twenty-dollar bill out of her bag and gave it to me.

I said, "Nope, I'm okay, Mom."

She insisted, "C'mon. Take it."

I needed the money, but I never wanted to financially burden my parents. I told her, "No mom, I am using my savings for my expenses." Mom proceeded to insert the bill into my polo shirt pocket. She hushed me before I could say another word. "Just take it. You might need it." I could do nothing else but take it. I said thanks again to Mom.

The truth was, the money helped cover my BART and bus fares. I only had $500 in pocket money when I arrived in the U.S. I had been scrimping so as not to deplete my savings too fast. It helped that Mom prepared lunchboxes for me. When she had extra money, she would hand me small bills to help me get by with my expenses.

I stepped out of the apartment, but after walking only a few meters, I noticed I had left my cell phone at home. I went back and used the extra key that Dad had given me to open the door. When I walked in, I saw Mom sitting on the sofa, her hands folded in prayer, quietly crying. When she saw me, she quickly looked the other way to hide her tears. She pretended to rub her eyes to wipe off the trickle of tears on her cheeks.

"Mom, I forgot my phone," I said to break the ice. I knew she had been fervently praying for me. She was concerned about my frustrations and worried that I was skipping meals to save money.

I assured Mom that I would be fine. "Mom, don't worry about me. I promise you I will be alright. I have your lunch in my backpack. I won't go hungry." She gently forced a smile and nodded in approval.

Then with all her motherly solicitude, she said, "If you need anything, just let me and your dad know. Don't let yourself go hungry, Frank." Holding back my tears, I whispered back, 'You bet. Thank you, Mommy."

Before I could leave, she asked, "What do you want for dinner?"

I shot back with, "*Binagoongan!*" (pork cooked in shrimp paste).

"Be home early tonight, then. Take care, my son," she said warmly.

Mom had always been concerned about her children's well-being. She was always concerned about the availability of food to us, and if we had been eating well. Perhaps because it was a reassuring thought that if you ate well, it followed that you were probably healthy and happy. Food was not only about pleasure to her. It was something essential. It was about life. Her passion for food translated to an expression of love and affection. Food had been a source of bonding that kept the family together.

I stepped out of the apartment walking into another day of job hunting with a smile on my face as I carried in my heart my Mom's thoughtfulness and endearing qualities. The sunny day came with the aroma of the lunchbox in my bag. It was only eight in the morning, but I already wanted to tuck away my lunch. It gave me another smile to think that I would never go hungry again while looking for a job. It also made me realize that whatever we, their children, do or got into, our parents were the most affected. If they saw us looking miserable, they would be more miserable than us. If they knew we are happy, they would be the happiest people on earth.

CHAPTER 3
FINDING WORK

After two months of looking for work, I finally found a job at an upscale senior living community called The Manor in Fremont, something like more than 40 miles from Concord.. The owner-director, Mr. Scott, employed me to work at the front desk and agreed to sponsor me for an H-1B work visa. I started working for The Manor immediately. In a month or two, the company evaluated my performance at work and thereafter, they asked me to file my application for work visa. Dad and Mom bankrolled the USCIS premium processing fee which was $2,130. I shouldered the initial payment for my immigration lawyer's fee which was $750, and the lawyer's evaluation fee for $250.

The front desk was opened 24 hours and provided concierge service to 90 residents living in their own swanky apartment units that were lined up in a well-appointed two-winged three-level building complex with a hotel-feel ambiance. The building also boasted of a spacious lobby and dining hall with elegant interior design. Breakfast, lunch, and dinner were served to residents in the dining hall or delivered to their units.

My duties included coordinating with different departments, checking on residents, facilitating emergency procedures, attending to visitors and inquiries, accepting rental payments, disseminating advisories to residents and staff, and making incident reports among other responsibilities. Besides my work at the front desk, I also helped at the activities department by contributing to the resident's newsletter and organizing special activities like mini-concerts, photo exhibits, and games.

As a new hire, I was assigned mostly graveyard shifts. As an employee, I was availed free lodging in one of the available apartment units for employees and a free meal during my shift. On my days off, I would go home to Concord to be with my parents. After my day off, I would pack dishes Mom had cooked that were good for two to three days and bring them with me back to The Manor for my meals.

While working at The Manor, I requested an extension of my stay as a tourist from the USCIS. I was given six months. When my extension expired, I applied for a second extension while my working visa was being processed. I was given another six months, which was the maximum I could get. When my second visitor extension expired, I still had not received my work visa. My application for the H-1B visa was later denied because my college degree did not correspond with my front desk position. I told Mr. Scott and my lawyer that I had overstayed my visa allowance. I was concerned that my presence was already illegal. They assured me that as long as my application for an H-1B visa was pending, I did not have to worry a bit and could go on working with the company. My lawyer filed an appeal twice with the USCIS, but nothing came out of it. Whether it was correct or not, I totally depended on whatever Mr. Scott and my lawyer told me.

My job at The Manor could have been the ideal opportunity for someone like me, who was starting to build a life in

America. But there was one setback that affected not only me, but the workforce in general. It was the fortyish Mr. Scott's volatile behavior. The owner-director, with his gentle and monk-like balding features, had a temper. He would go into a fit of rage for the pettiest reasons. He castigated employees with his insulting and downgrading choices of words. He yelled at employees without mercy. Generous with his swearing, he would scream profanities like he was firing stray bullets that flew all over.

Mr. Scott would not put up with the smallest incompetence or offense from his employees. If he was in a bad mood, we would see heads rolling in a snap of a finger. It did not matter whether you were in a managerial position, the rank and file, a long-time employee, or one who had been working for only a day. It seemed like he was in a constant hunt for employees to fire at his pleasure like a savage wolf sniffing for his prey. We were all at his mercy and clung to our jobs. All employees kept an eye out for his wrath to save their necks.

The firing practices at The Manor booted out many hardworking and talented employees who had contributed greatly to the company. Our At-Will employment was used heavily as a platform to fire employees, under the guise of effective management and organizational efficiency. The company was like implementing unwritten or unofficial rules and were like hyping on loopholes or booby-trapping employees so they can fire them for minor offenses like one-time tardiness, instead of recognizing employees' performance, productivity, and talent. Many employees had quit their jobs because they felt they were being treated badly and could not bear the undue tension and pressure in the workplace. In addition to that, employees were overworked because of understaffing. They were given workloads that were supposed to be performed by other workers.

The management team was helpless in the face of demoralization in the rank and file. All of them were just following the rules and Mr. Scott's orders. Another thing that exacerbated the situation at work was Mr. Scott's minions who snitched on employees to gain his favor. His minions were good as trolls who were always on the lookout for employees who are committing mistakes. The company employees were good-hearted people who enjoyed pleasant working and personal relationships with each other. Because the minions tattled with fake, baseless, or exaggerated stories that surprisingly, Mr. Scott believed, it wreaked havoc in the relationships between employees, instigating buck-passing, misunderstandings, confusion, division, betrayals, and conspiracies among some of them.

Our sales and promotion pitch that bannered on compassionate and caring senior living was far-fetched. Mr. Scott did not really care about the residents' welfare. All he cared about was profit. On the other hand, during the times he was in good mood, he was the most generous and equable person in the office. He would give presents to employees and treat his management team to dinner. His smiles would be displayed the entire day, prompting everyone to wish he stayed that way every day. If Mr. Scott had only placed a premium on human values and sensibilities, and respected the employees' dignity and self-worth, I would say he was a good boss despite his peculiarities and mood swings.

I shared those stories at work with my parents. I told them that it was okay to be cornered and corrected for your mistakes at work but to make it like a witch-hunt was irrational and unfair, considering that their workforce was comprised of hardworking and dedicated people. Mom advised me to keep working hard and follow the rules in order not to be singled out. She reminded me to keep on praying and be good to all my coworkers. Dad gave me his advice. "Give no time to intrigues and backstabbing but learn how to defend and protect yourself. Just do your job and do it right and do it well."

During my training period at The Manor, I almost got fired because I was not computer literate. I had never had any interest in computers. Since I had hardly ever used one, my knowledge about them was almost nil. My job at The Manor happened to require knowledge about a lot of computer applications. I asked Karla, my supervisor, to teach me but she gave me hasty and uncoordinated instructions that left me untaught. She gave me a cursory orientation of my duties and responsibilities and did not give me an employee handbook, a standard office procedure in the company, until she was reminded of by an officemate. After that, she overzealously snitched on me about my incompetence to Mr. Travis, the front desk manager. It was alright if she reported me, but she should have at least given me the benefit of the doubt or let me prove myself first before she hurriedly did that.

Mr. Travis immediately tested my computer knowledge and naturally, I failed. He then gave me a chance to learn all the computer applications in one week by giving me a simplified manual. Karla failed to give me that manual even if she knew that would be a helpful guide to my learning. The manual contained illustrations and step-by-step instructions to follow in the applications. Retaining my job depended on whether I met the mark.

Burning the midnight oil, I rigorously reviewed the

handout and practiced while at work. Within three days, I was already using the computer on my own. I had learned to do data entry, file reports, MS Word, and how to send out communications among other things. It was easy. I had just not been given the right head start. When the manager retested me, I confidently passed the test, feeling like I was an instant tech savvy. I was thankful that I was given a fair chance to catch up and make good. In a reversal of fortune, Karla was fired after three months for incompetence.

As I made progress at work, Dad and Mom bought me a brand new laptop to help me become more adept with the computer. Some years later, when my first computer became outdated, they bought me another brand new one.

CHAPTER 4
BAPTISM BY FIRE

When Dad and Mom were fresh off the boat, they had also worked at an upscale senior living facility called The Haven in Walnut Creek. That was their first job. Dad worked as a waiter while Mom worked as a caregiver. They told me a story about something that happened right after they got hired. Dad was carrying a tray of food and drinks over to some of the residents in the dining hall at lunchtime when he tripped and dropped the tray, which created a loud clanging sound and messed up the carpet in the dining area. Dad's slip caught the attention of all the residents and visitors alike. He saw his supervisor shaking his head in disgust. He had never felt so embarrassed in his entire life. He was very apologetic as he patiently cleaned up the mess. Mom wanted to help Dad clean up, but she had her hands full assisting the residents.

Mom was holding in her emotions as she finished her tasks with the residents. As soon as she was done, she excused herself and went into a corner to let her tears pour out. Mom naturally took pity on Dad. She knew that he was not used to doing menial jobs. He was used to giving orders—not taking them. Mom knew, however, that she could not use that rationale to understand and explain why he had committed that misstep. There was no need to explain it anyway. She knew that it was not Dad's fault. It was just an honest mistake. It was just that they were not used to getting undue attention during an embarrassing incident. Mom was showing her empathy for Dad, and felt like their life in America was demeaning and different from the one they had in the Philippines.

In due time, Dad and Mom learned to face the music and rise from their fall. They had figured out how to overcome their baptism by fire. They learned to face the challenges while they adjusted to a new life in their adopted land. What kept them going was their partnership, which was supportive and complementary. That was how they drew strength and courage from each other.

When Dad's supervisor talked to him about the incident, Dad bargained with him to allow him ample time to shape up and learn the ropes since he had just started. In due time, Dad made good on his word. He not only made remarkable progress at The Haven, but also in every job he took thereafter. From his job at The Haven, he went on to work as a clerk at the United States Postal Service, an office assistant at DMV, a handyman at EZ-8 Motel, a retail sales associate/cashier at Target, a retail sales associate at K-Mart, a bellman at Hilton, until he found a good-paying job as a distribution clerk at John Muir Medical Center.

When my parents migrated to the U.S., they went through culture shock for a brief period. It took them some effort to adjust to a new lifestyle. To be uprooted and re-planted in a cold, strange land that was to be their new home was doubly challenging to them. They had to be tough to be able to face the struggles, loneliness, and changes in their new life in America. In the Philippines, they had housemaids who did everything for them. In the U.S., they were their own housemaids and had to do everything for themselves.

Because of their age and health condition (both were diabetic and Mom had a heart condition), they were not as keen, at first, to look for a job. Like most senior citizens, they were technologically behind. They were not proficient in computer which was one factor that slashed their competitive edge and lessened their chances of getting a job they wanted. They were forced to take a variety of jobs so they could start building their own careers and survive. If they did not work, there was nowhere else for them to go and no food on the table.

When Mom was younger, she was given the opportunity to work as a nurse at a hospital in Chicago. She did not take it, choosing family and maternal responsibility instead. We were still kids then and needed her personal care and attention. She was a working mother, having a full-time job as a clinical instructor in a local university. She was a mother and wife round-the-clock to her family. It was a hard decision for her because her career choice would also be a great factor affecting her children's future. But whatever the pros and cons were that her decision gave rise to, she never regretted it because she was fulfilled and happy just to be with the family she loved.

In the Philippines, even if my parents did not work, they had earnings from the properties they owned which would pay the bills. The pressure in the U.S. made their lifestyle quite different from what they were used to back home. As they faced their struggles in America, they had to deal with the reality of taking or not taking what was right in front of them. They had relatives and friends who helped them along the way, but their struggle rested mainly in their own hands. They had to make their own decisions and see where that led them.

To give support to Dad, Mom strived on her own to build an ideal and comfortable life for them in the U.S. She went on to have a brief stint as a caregiver at The Haven. Then she worked as a retail sales associate at Target and later at K-Mart.

I had known my mother as someone who kept a low profile. Feeling concerned about how she was coping with her job, which was so different from her job as a teacher or dean in the Philippines, I once asked her, "Mom, are you enjoying your work?"

She said, "Yes, I get to exercise while working. I'm good at my work. It's decent, and I'm enjoying and earning at the same time and have many friends there."

I innocently queried her, "What if one of your students saw you working there? How would you react?"

Mom quipped briefly in a gentle and humble manner that was characteristic of her. "The question should not be how would I react, because I am happy and proud of what I'm doing. It should be how do I think my students would react? I am good at my job. Whatever they might think about it, that's okay with me, but I don't think my students would say anything. I am confident they would just be as happy to see me as I would be to see them."

Mom remained attached to many of her former students and faculty members. She was mighty proud and happy of their successes and achievements. When she was still teaching, she was somewhat strict with her students. Many of them were scared to take her class. Mom's objective was to make her students get serious about their studies because once they start working, they would be taking care of the sick and saving lives. She thought that they should be well-equipped for that mission. Besides, Mom would volunteer to say that their parents worked hard and sacrificed a lot to be able to send them to school. Eventually, many students thanked her and became fond of her. She taught Psychiatric Nursing among other subjects.

My first Christmas and New Year's Eve celebrations in the U.S. were spent at work. It was also my first Christmas and New Year's alone and away from my family. It was December 2003. Dad and Mom decided to postpone their *Noche Buena* (Christmas Eve dinner) and hold it instead when I got home on my day off. In the meantime, they had a small holiday dinner to celebrate the occasion. We arranged the same thing for *Media Noche* (New Year's Eve dinner). My wife and son in the Philippines had their celebrations ahead because of the time difference. The time in the Philippines is sixteen hours ahead of California.

That Christmas Eve, I was tired from the day's work. As soon as I got off from work at 11:30 p.m., I went straight up to my apartment. I did not have time to buy food for my Christmas Eve dinner. I feasted on leftover sardines and steamed rice from the fridge. In my bed, I played a CD of the Kenny Loggins song "Celebrate Me Home." It spoke of one's longing to be home for the holidays. As I listened to the song, I stared at the dark ceiling and felt lonely. I missed my family. I played the song over and over again throughout the night until I dozed off. I woke up to the ringing sound of the alarm clock. It was 6 a.m. on Christmas Day. I wished myself a happy and gastronomically pleasing Christmas day. I dragged myself out of bed and showered quickly to make it to work before 7 a.m.

When I started my shift, the elegant but cozy lobby was

filled with merriment as families came in droves to fetch residents for family gatherings. Residents who went on holiday trips or family vacations had left yesterday or days before. The few residents who chose to spend the holiday at The Manor were visited by their families who came bearing gifts and goodies. The flurry of activities slowed down before lunchtime as most residents and their families had left. The lobby emptied but for some residents who had no visitors. They opted to sit around a little longer, waiting to see if the next visitor coming through the entrance door was for them. Just like everyone else, they longed to kiss and hug someone. They longed to hold the hand of someone special to them. They longed to greet and talk to someone. They each missed someone they loved and cared for.

Seeing families happy together around them pierced deep into their loneliness and longing. It made them feel more alone and forgotten. As the sound of Christmas carols played in the spacious lobby that was decorated for the holidays, and the lights in the Christmas tree glittered, their lonely eyes revealed all the pain that contradicted the spirit of the holiday season. I only had empathy for them.

All the residents and I longed to be with our families. Especially on Christmas, where part of its true meaning gravitated around family and relationships. There were varied circumstances that isolated one from one's family. I was wondering if mine were just the price I had to pay to pursue my dreams.

My first Christmas alone and away from home crystallized my thoughts that without your loved ones by your side, your enchantment during the holidays would only be superficial. It would only be a feast to the eyes and the stomach, but not the heart. I longed for my family because that is where I belong and feel love. My family is what made me whole and fulfilled. I prayed that someday, my family would cross the bridge that would reunite us and never separate us again.

The message of Christmas has always been the same from the beginning up to present times. Jesus was born to spread love and peace and bring hope and joy to mankind. If we look around us, the gift of Christmas is what we already have. It is found in the family, where there is a bounty of love. It is what makes a home. It teaches us to love and respect others. And it is not only the love that we receive from the family that counts. It is also the love that you give yourself. This is the most priceless gift we can ever get. It is the biggest blessing in our lives, and we do not have to spend a cent for it. Many of us fail to see it because we have been setting the wrong priorities in our lives. Mankind's intimacy with materialism and utmost respect for money has overshadowed our values for family and home, which are far more important than all the material wealth we could ever acquire in our lives.

CHAPTER 5
STENT

In 2006, Mom had undergone a stent procedure. As explained by Mom's doctor, Dr. Kauffman, a reputable cardiologist in the Bay Area, it is a minimally invasive procedure that involves inserting a tiny metal or plastic tube into a narrowed or blocked artery to improve blood flow into the heart. At first, Dad and I took a negative view about the procedure. It was not because we had questions about the doctor's qualifications. We personally knew the doctor and could attest that he was one of the best surgeons in the Bay Area. We were confident he would take good care of Mom. What Dad and I were worried about was Mom's age and well-being. We had this inexplicable fear that no matter how good a doctor Dr. Kauffman was, if something went wrong, it could be fatal for Mom who was frail and old.

With a lot of fear in our hearts, Dad and I eventually made up our minds that the procedure would be good for Mom, despite the risks involved. The procedure went on as scheduled at the John Muir Health, Concord Medical Center. On that day, Dad and I anxiously waited in the waiting room. Some minutes passed, we saw a commotion in the operating room. It looked like there was an exigency with the nurses rushing here and there. We tried to be calm until we heard the term "Code Blue' from one of the nurses. It sent shivers down our spines because of our earlier fears about the procedure. Dad prayed hard for Mom's safety and broke down in tears. His anxiety got the best of him. In all my life, it was the first time I had ever seen Dad crying. With bated breath, we waited for anyone who can tell us what was going on.

Finally, the unassuming Dr. Kauffman came out of the operating room looking tired and spent. The fortyish, tall, and heavy doctor immediately approached Dad and said, "God is good. Mom is doing fine. You can see her in a moment." What Dr. Kauffman told us gave us great relief. We thanked the Almighty God that Mom had come out safe and alive from the procedure.

We later found out that during the time when there was a commotion while the procedure was going on, Mom had become critical when she started to bleed excessively and had unexpected cardiac arrest. The medical team did their best in their resuscitation efforts. The good doctor told us he had prayed for God's help to save mom's life and for a successful procedure. When Mom was revived and declared stable, he took it as a divine intervention. Since then, every time Dr. Kauffman saw my Mom for a checkup, he would hug her and exclaim, "My miracle mom, Maria."

My mother was blessed with a new lease on life. She recovered gradually and impatiently. Impatiently, because she could not wait to get back to eating regular food. She had already reacquired her sense of taste, but was not yet allowed to eat her favorite foods. She fought cravings and temptations, but there were a few times she would give in.

Mom loved food. She really enjoyed eating. That was one of her passions and joys. When she ate, she stayed at the table for hours, chewing slowly and savoring every single bite. After a meal, she would bring out a variety of desserts from the refrigerator and delight herself by savoring each of them. Afterwards, she would take out packaged snacks from the kitchen cabinet like peanuts, chips, chocolate bars, and cookies to nibble after dessert. After Mom had undergone the stent procedure, we tolerated her teeny-weeny bites of anything to satisfy her cravings and nourish her back to health. Dad and I would keep an eye on her to make sure she was still within limits.

As a former practicing nurse, Mom knew how to control or discipline herself as she recuperated. She acted responsibly as a patient. She would readily acquiesce if we reminded her of her mandated diet or restrictions. She had a very pleasant disposition.

There were times Mom would be in a playful mood. She would take more food than she was allowed to eat. I would then blithely chide her for doing that. She would react by placing her index finger in front of her pursed lips to coax me not to tell Dad. With an impish smile, she would rib me by saying, "Keep your mouth sealed." It was very comical. The two of us would end up breaking into laughter together.

Deep inside, I pitied my mother. I wanted her to enjoy life at her age. I thought depriving her of the little pleasures was repressive. On the other hand, I knew her food restrictions were for her own good. Knowing that, I decided to use reverse psychology on myself about it. Whenever I saw her control her appetite or fight her cravings, I cheer up instead of pitying her. I would look at it as a sign of recovery and tell myself that in a little more time, Mom would be back to enjoying again the food she loved to her heart's desire, just like what she used to do before the procedure.

Given the second chance at life, Mom continued to recover. She did not totally get her agility back, but she was able to return to her regular activities. One by one, she was able to go back to cooking, shopping at the mall and the supermarket, taking walks, and attending Mass every morning with neighbors. Much to her delight, she had also started eating regular food albeit in moderation. She had gone back to enjoying her favorite dishes. In restaurants, she would order anything she liked but she would request her food to be less salty, oily, and sweet.

Mom was not able to go back to work at K-Mart, though. Because of her long hiatus and inability to endure physically stressful tasks, the management had to let her go. Mom took it as her retirement, although she never received any benefits for her dedicated and untiring service to the company. She was told the reason was because she was not a permanent employee.

All along, Mom had thought she was a permanent employee after working there for eight years. If she was not permanent, why had not the management bothered or had the heart to change her employment status so she could receive benefits considering that she had been working there for a long time? They never advised Mom if she needed to fill out an application form to become permanent or if she needed to do other steps to avail of benefits when she retired. There was not a single initiative coming from them. There was not one iota of concern nor a tinge of support coming from them. Was it a built-in system to avoid paying benefits?

Whether mom was permanent or not, we have nothing against K-Mart. Mom worked there for a long time because she thinks it was a good company to work for. Whether mom would get benefits or not, it did not matter to us anymore. We appreciated it both ways, but I could have appreciated it better if the management had realized that they could have done better than making old employees look like coffee cups to be disposed of after they had used them. Dad and Mom decided to just forget it and concentrate on mom's recovery. Mom never got anything from K-Mart but the Lord had given her the biggest benefit that she could ever get in her life. Her second life.

CHAPTER 6
RECOVERY

My parents celebrated their fiftieth wedding anniversary in June 2006. To mark this milestone and Mom's recovery, we planned for a bigger celebration. Mom, however, opted to have a small and simple but meaningful celebration. We ended up hosting an intimate dinner for twelve guests in a Chinese restaurant in Walnut Creek. On that day, Dad and Mom were the quintessential lovebirds who were grateful to the Lord for blessing them with a long-lasting love and marriage.

In a span of a few years after their fiftieth wedding anniversary, Mom started to become forgetful. Dad and I mistook it as a normal sign of aging. We were astounded one day when Mom suddenly seemed to have manifested cognitive impairment and memory loss. We learned about it when she went to church by herself one time. The church was in walking distance, just three blocks away. After the Mass, she got disoriented and could not find her way back home. She could not call Dad because she had left her cell phone in the apartment. She came across a gas station and asked for directions and got even more confused. The gas station had no public phone. She went over and stood on a corner outside the station, crying, trying to think of what to do next. Fortunately, a good Samaritan noticed her and drove her safely home.

There was another incident that happened when Mom went to the store four blocks from the apartment. Walking to the store was part of her walking regimen after her stent procedure. She was able to get back home, but it had taken her some time to compose herself and recall her way back. Mom's doctor said she was in the early stage of Alzheimer's Disease, a progressive neurological disorder that destroys memory and other important mental functions. We told her not to go out anymore without us accompanying her.

As the years passed, we noticed other changes in Mom's health. Her reflexes slackened. She spilled her coffee on the table, dropped plates while washing them in the sink and tripped over and fell on the floor many times, even if she moved and walked slowly and carefully. She also developed cataracts, poor eyesight, and hearing impairment.

To push Mom to fend off the advancement of Alzheimer's Disease, Dad and I pressured her to do more mental and physical exercises. To prevent the occurrence of accidents, we urged her to hold things with her two hands and be more cautious when walking. When we are reminding her, we would say it loudly to make sure she heard us.

One morning, the sound of smoke alarm woke me up from my sleep in the living room. I quickly got up from the sofa to smoke that was starting to engulf the room. I saw the kettle blackened from the small fire that had been lit under it on the stove. The kettle had dried up of water. Mom came out of the bathroom, shocked. I took a kitchen towel, soaked it with water, and put out the fire with it. Then I opened the window up wide to release the smoke in the living room.

It turned out that Mom had switched on the stove to boil water. She had gone to the bathroom and entirely forgot that she was boiling water. Dad had left for work earlier. It was good that I was at home at that time. I was shocked, but Mom was the most shocked and upset of all. She could not believe that she had made the kind of mistake that she had been doing her best to avoid. She had always been very careful about everything she did. I comforted her by telling her not to worry about it because I knew it was not her fault, but I reminded her to continue being extra careful in whatever she was doing, even if she experiences lapses and mistakes.

What happened to Mom was a manifestation of the disease. I had heard similar stories from other families who had an Alzheimer's parent. Some of the stories were even worse, depending on how much the disease had progressed on each person. There were also similar stories coming from parents who do not have Alzheimer's, but because of old age, had become forgetful. I know I will be old and forgetful too someday which was why I understood what Mom was going through. I advised her to use the stove only when Dad and I were around the house to avoid accidents. She fully understood that Alzheimer's was taking a toll on her. She was hurting and felt bad that no matter how much she tried to remember things and be careful, she would still forget things and commit blunders.

Mom usually kept her worries to herself because she did not want to disturb people, although she had her vulnerable moments too. One time, she poured her heart out to Dad and me. She told us about her frustrations, that no matter what she did, she felt like she was gradually slipping and becoming inutile. She felt like a burden to us. She added that she was sad that nobody really understood how she felt.

Mom's surge of anxiety struck a chord in Dad and me. The truth was, we wanted her to get back on track and be safe. Dad and I always meant well, but sometimes maybe we took the wrong approach and offended Mom's sensibilities. Perhaps sometimes we were tactless because we did not realize how sensitive Mom had become as she came to grips with her condition and old age.

There was a time my heart sank when I saw Mom wistfully sitting on the sofa in the living room. She was looking far out the window, her eyes melancholy. I knew she was reflecting on her life as she was immersed in deep thought.

I wanted to tell Mom that we would not pressure or nag her anymore. That she did not have to adjust to or keep up with us. I wanted to tell her that I love her. Regrettably, I could not articulate my sentiments. I was fearful that I might say it wrong, and that Mom would misinterpret what I told her, hurting her feelings more in the process. It stopped me from taking the chance to say anything comforting at all to her.

In hindsight. I thought Mom really did not need any explanation on my part as she usually took things with wisdom and understanding. I think all she really needed was for Dad and me to be beside her to make her feel that she was loved and important, and that we cared for her and would always take care of her. I tried my best to be there for Mom, but I believe I could have done more. For Dad, he had always been there for Mom with full support and understanding. However, I thought Dad and I fell short on expressing our love for her in spoken words. I knew Mom knows that we love her. She did not need to hear reassuring words from us. Still, I believe telling people that you love them is a course of action that inspires, reassures, and heals. Perhaps it was a disadvantage that Dad was not extra showy or expressive of his feelings in spoken words, just like I do. I get complacent to think that Dad and Mom probably could have discussed mom's worries more exhaustively in their private moments together. I believe Dad could have expressed himself better in spoken words to Mom when it was just the two of them together, knowing that they have always been so supportive and complementary in their relationship.

When I came to the U.S., I felt my parents looked up to me somewhat as their representative or connection to their distant family. Dad and Mom had direct and frequent telephone calls and messaging with every member of the family. However, it was I who provided a face, a physical presence, a window, an extension, or a personification to their longing for a whole and complete family. The years that I lived with them provided a sample of a domestic family experience that they held precious in their hearts. It provided a picture of what it was like at home back in the days when we were all together. Our lives together in the U.S. became their conduit to the family life and relationships that they had in the Philippines.

Unfortunately, I was not a good representative. I was spending too much time earning a living and working hard to keep my job and get a work visa. In doing so, I forgot about finding enough time to be with my parents. I get to bond with my parents on my days off, but there were times when I had to cancel out our dinner and movie dates. They were disappointed because they always looked forward to going out with me. I was grateful that they never complained. They always tried to understand.

CHAPTER 7

AXED

During the long time that I had worked at The Manor, I was promoted to front desk supervisor. Things were running smoothly until one day, Mr. Scott noticed I was sporting a long and tousled hair. He said he wanted his staff to adhere to the company's policy or best practices on personal grooming and told me to get a haircut. On that day, I had so much work to do that I had to work late to get it done. By the time I was through, the barber shops had closed. I knew it was my fault not to follow a simple instruction, but I was hoping I could explain the reason why I failed to get a haircut. I gave priority to my job and did not want to bungle it. I came to work the next day with uncut hair, and was let go for that reason. I was not given the chance to explain.

It was around 2006. I looked for a job in the same door-to-door manner. The economic growth in the U.S. had slowed down and there was a dearth of job openings. I was out of job for about six months. I called back The Manor to reapply. Maybe because of my good record, I was rehired, but was assigned to work at their larger senior living community in Redwood City called The Garden. It had about 190 residents living in their own cozy apartments in a ten-story building with similar facilities and services provided at The Manor. In a few months, I was promoted to front desk manager.

Everything went smoothly for more than a year until one day, I was fired for coming to work two minutes late. It was the first quarter of 2008. I went back home to my parents carrying two large bags of clothes and personal items, a large plastic bag containing pots and pans, kitchenware, plates, cutlery, and another plastic bag containing books and leftover snacks.

"I lost my job." I announced the bad news.

"What happened?" Dad queried.

"I was two minutes late when I came to work," I replied.

"That is unbelievable." Dad was pissed off.

"I also lost my employment petition." I announced the other bad news.

"How could they do that to you?" Dad was fuming.

Mom was disenchanted but remained collected and compassionate. She was confident that I would be able to bounce back. The burden was easier to carry when I was at home because that was where I felt a strong support system. I lost my job, but I had no worries. I had good food to eat and a comfortable place to sleep. Dad and Mom were always there, ready to catch me if I fall. The load was less, because my parents were quietly carrying it with me, without expecting repayment or reward, and without seeking the limelight.

That year, the U.S. was experiencing one of its worst economic declines in its history, brought about by the subprime mortgage crisis and other factors. The financial crisis in the U.S. later ushered in a severe worldwide depression. Many people lost their jobs, and jobs were painfully scarce. The timing of losing my job struck me with uncertainty. I had no job amid the economic instability. I had lost the employment petition that I had been waiting for a long time to legalize my stay. It was now clear to me that I was hope-lessly thrown into the category of undocumented alien. I was down, and back to square one.

When I called my wife, I sadly told her that I had no longer had a work and employment petition. She told me not to lose heart, consoling me by telling me that she was sure there would be other opportunities that would come my way. I found myself explaining to her that I was not frus-trated about losing my job because I was ready to look for another one. But I was worried about the monthly remit-tance I was going to send them. I did not want it disrupted. I did not want to be a failure to them. For a few months, I used my savings to send money to them at a reduced amount from my usual remittance. I promised my wife that I would find a job before I ran out of my savings. She told me not to worry about her and Ken. She assured me that they would be okay.

It was ironic that it was alright with me to lose my job. I had always wanted to leave there anyway. Even if the em-ployment opportunities were grim, I know I could eventu-ally find another job. I had always been a determined person. I know I would find my way out of my worries and achieve my goal.

I stood firm on my principles in life. When I was fired, I asked the point of view of Mr. Travis, who maintained an open communication line with his staff, about the com-pany's draconian method of terminating employment. I know that I needed to be aware of and follow company poli-cies. I know that I had an At-Will employment with them. But I also know that At-Will employment should not be abused the way they abused it.

I know that management were just following Mr. Scott's

orders and company rules about terminating employees. The management people, even if they had sympathy for employees, could not fight for them because of fear of getting the axe themselves. It did not matter if the employee was an asset and had contributed considerably to the company. The company had such low regard toward their employees, that they could fire them for the most unreasonable or trivial grounds like they were just swatting flies. The company was apathetic to employees' plight.

A minion heard what I was saying, and I had no idea I was sending the wrong message. The minion quickly tipped off Mr. Scott, who apparently was given the wrong information. On my way out of Mr. Travis' office, I ran into Mr. Scott in the hallway. He warned me that he would report me to ICE (Immigration and Customs Enforcement) because I am undocumented. Back then, I was neophyte and ignorant about the ways of life. All I had ever wanted was to work to support my family and nothing more. I did not want trouble. I was not complaining. I was not picking a fight. I was simply asking, not questioning, and imparting in the most courteous manner, my unsolicited opinion about a company rule. What could I say about Mr. Scott's scare tactics and callousness?

It had always been my trait that if someone had done me wrong, I would try to stretch my patience and understanding as much as possible. I would also reflect to see what I had done wrong myself. I inherited that trait from my mother. But when my patience hit the limit, I would fight with all my strength. That was what I inherited from my father.

Mr. Scott had been more tolerant with me through the years that I had worked with them. Because of that, I showed forbearance and respect to him in return. However, the years of putting up with and witnessing so much oppression and degradation in the office had shattered my innocence and ignorance. It had opened my eyes to fight and survive in a mean and deceptive environment. I tried to politely respond to Mr. Scott's careless and mindless warning. "Mr. Scott, don't you realize that you were my employer? It's kind of funny that if you report me, you will also be reporting yourself and dragging yourself down with me." Mr. Scott was having a good day. He simply showed no reaction.

Mr. Scott had his reasons why he ran his company and handled his people the way he did. He had a prerogative to set his policy or rule for his own company. He had a vision and goal to achieve. He just forgot to balance his decisions and actions. He was drastic on his employees. He forgot that building and running his business was not unilateral. It needed the help of people, especially his employees. I had hoped someday this realization would boomerang at his conscience and enlightened him to see if what he had been doing merited accolade or flak, was fair or unfair, or was on the right track or derailed.

The anxiety of losing my job juxtaposed my relief and gladness to end a period of torment. I was breathless for the opportunity to start anew. I walked away from my job with my dignity and self-respect intact. I felt like a free man walking away from exploitation and denigration. I had held onto my job because I needed a job and paycheck. It was time that I get a fulfilling and rewarding job where I get equal access to learn and grow, improve my skills and personality, achieve my goals, and regarded as a contributor, partner or team member to the company's achievements, objective and success.

I applied for a job using the same approach. I went knocking door-to-door. It was harder this time because of the economic situation. It was persistence, sacrifice, and prayers that kept me going. My parents worried about my being out-of-status. They encouraged me to look for another employer/sponsor and advised me to consult immigration lawyers to discuss ways to address my immigration problem.

When I was a kid, I had envisioned America to be something like Disneyland. But when I worked and lived in the U.S., my perception changed. I had seen and experienced America's other side. As in any country, you have the good and the bad side. It just depends on how you take to and adjust to those sides. As a stranger trying to find his place under the sun, I faced the harsh reality and desolation along the way. I bitterly struggled to survive. I was lucky I had my parents who supported me and some people who encouraged me to carry on. You either make it or break it. You either win it or lose it. How you handle the struggle is in your own hands. I woke up losing my Disneyland dream, and instead, found myself looking at the reality of life where there is endless rat race and grueling struggle to survive in any place in the world.

I love America as I love my homeland, the Philippines. America is a great country. I believe in its democratic ideals and value for humanity. I believe in its promise of equality and opportunity. That was one reason why we adopted America as our new home. My parents and I struggled hard to be a part of that greatness and endeavored to integrate ourselves into mainstream society. We broke our backs for many years. That was how we knew we could contribute to the country. We believed that the nation's greatness and bounties came from every blood, sweat and tears of working people.

Like my parents before me, I had my own struggles while trying to build a life and chase my dreams. After my stint with the senior living communities, I found work at Jack in the Box in Concord through a friend's referral. I worked with Filipinos and Latinos, and we got along well with each other. I became a shift supervisor there. I was offered a management position at a different location but I rejected it because of its distance from Concord.

Then I worked as a waiter in a Chinese/Japanese restaurant in Walnut Creek. The owner was a good man, but he had his moods. If business was slow, he tended to flare up for the slightest reason. His restaurant was small and most of the time was packed. I worked as a dishwasher first before I became a waiter. All my coworkers were older and spoke very little English. I had a hard time catching up and coping there because there was nobody who could help me whenever I had questions about the food and their system of operation. I was able to learn by observing.

I left the Walnut Creek restaurant when a sushi chef-friend asked me to help him run his sushi restaurant that he was opening in Brentwood. Another sushi chef-friend asked me to work in his trendy sushi place that he had just opened in the Piedmont/Montclair area in Oakland, but I had already said yes to my friend in Brentwood. I worked at my friend's restaurant in Brentwood for more than a year. It was a successful venture as it became a very busy restaurant. During my stint at the Brentwood restaurant, my former boss at the Chinese/Japanese restaurant in Walnut Creek called to ask if I wanted to work for him again. I went back to work as a waiter for him because his place was closer to my parent's apartment. Several employees I worked with before had left and had been replaced by new ones. Nevertheless, just like before, it always packed the customers in.

After working back in the Walnut Creek restaurant for about two years, another friend opened a Chinese/Japanese restaurant, in Rockridge. It was around 2014. My friend Ron offered me the position of restaurant manager. I did not accept it because I did not have any prior experience or training in managing a restaurant. I told him I was good to work as a waiter.

When he opened the restaurant, I was surprised when Ron introduced me to the employees and customers as the manager. I could not do anything but to accept it. As I tackled my new responsibilities, Ron taught me the ins and outs of the restaurant business. The work was taxing as it demanded personal attention and myriad responsibilities. Ron and I worked together to realize his vision of a restaurant with a welcoming and comfortable ambiance where family and friends could feel at home while they enjoyed good food. As I learned while working, I knew I would be a good fit. I worked in that restaurant for a long time.

The name of the restaurant was Dynasty. I still have a vignette of it when I first entered its doors. I thought I heard a gong being struck that echoed through its walls. I was blown away by its interior as it offered a glimpse of Chinese culture. The foyer had a small set of carved wooden Chinese period furniture with a large Buddha statue sitting on a varnished wood console table placed in a corner of a wall to accentuate it. Inside the dining area, there were sixteen regular-sized square tables covered in red tablecloths that could accommodate sixty-four people. Each table had four chairs upholstered in red velvet fabric. The walls were painted red and gold and there were many picture frames hanging on them adorned with Chinese characters. The ceilings were graced with red lanterns of different sizes. Inside the cashier's counter, there was a carved wooden altar continuously lit by small electric candles.

My friend took over the restaurant from its former owners who had decided to focus their attention on their restaurant in Antioch. One by one, the former owners took back their Chinese decors, furniture and tablecloth that left Dynasty almost bare of Chinese representation but for a few red paper lanterns and frames with Chinese characters.

At Dynasty, most of my coworkers were older Chinese people who spoke little English. Whenever I had to ask them something, they would politely shake their heads or say "little English." The younger ones, though, were fluent in the English language. Whether or not they spoke English, it did not become a barrier or deterrent to connect with them. Interacting through signs and actions was the method I used to communicate with them. We translated those signs and actions into words. That process led us to swap English and Chinese words which enriched our bilingual vocabularies. It was also a unique way to bond with each other.

My friend consistently mentored me as I continued to learn from my daily work experience. He had worked as a sushi chef in a few different restaurants before and had managed a restaurant for a time. As I became more confident in managing the restaurant, I became more grounded as well in other areas of restaurant operations including customer service, handling customer complaints, troubleshooting, waitstaff service training, and staff development programs.

The period that I worked at Dynasty immersed me into Chinese culture. It opened a door for me to learn a foreign culture and its traditions. I got to taste authentic Chinese dishes prepared according to tradition from different regions in China. Traditional Chinese cuisine is far different from the fusion food that are usually offered in many Chinese restaurants. Fusion foods are reinvented to cater to American taste and replace traditional ingredients with the available local ingredients. My Chinese friends told me that most of the dishes and products that we offered in our restaurant were unknown in China. That included the popular fortune cookies that we gave gratis when we bring the bill to the table. The early Chinese immigrants themselves most likely conceptualized and introduced those foods and products in America.

My Dynasty job enabled me to experience first-hand how my coworkers celebrated the Chinese New Year in America, with all the food and the giving of ang pao, which is a red envelope or packet where the giver puts money to be given as a gift. The Chinese in the Philippines held similar Chinese New Year's celebrations with holiday foods and ang pao. Filipino-Chinese have Lauriat, a banquet consisting of at least 8 to 10 sumptuous dishes. Lauriat came from the word lao diat, which means "special occasion" from the original Fookien dialect. As people became busier in modern times, lauriats had become more of a lavish catering event or held at plush restaurants and hotels, instead of being cooked and celebrated at home.

I consider Dynasty as a microcosm of the Chinese way of life and culture. In cosmopolitan California, you get many opportunities to bump into various cultures. The Chinese culture is one of the more dominant cultures to discover. The people of the Chinese diaspora were able to preserve, practice, introduce and promote their rich culture in their adopted land. My managerial stint at Dynasty became a culinary and cultural journey as well that reconnected me to my Chinese lineage.

After a long day in the restaurant, I would go home tired. Coworkers who lived in Concord would usually give me a ride home or drive me to the nearest BART Station at work where I can take a train going to the Concord BART station. From there, I would drag my feet to walk home while assessing the gains and losses of the day. When it was freezing outside, I would arrive home quivering from the cold. When I got caught in a downpour, I would find myself drenched and dripping with rainwater. I was always vigilant for suspicious characters that I met on the street that might cause trouble as I walk home but I was also ready to throw a punch or ran off for safety with my weary feet. I was fortunate I had always been safe in my daily commute. At home, I would rest my aching back, sore feet and legs, and weary mind in my sleep so I would be ready to work the next day.

Because of the stress, sometimes I would get indisposed. There was a time I developed severe coughing that lasted many days longer than usual. Back then, I had entertained thoughts that I might have contracted tuberculosis. My parents attempted to bring me to the hospital, but I put my foot down. I was tired of hospitals. When I was a kid, I was sickly. I was in and out of the hospital. Since I insisted on recuperating at home, my mother would check in on me and administer my medicines. I told her I could take care of myself, but she insisted on checking on me, even in the dead of the night. Thank God, I was up and about in very little time. I just needed to rest my exhausted body and mind sometimes.

Although the various jobs that I took in America might

be considered small achievements, for someone who started with nothing, I was proud of what I had done. It was all the result of hard work and sacrifices. With faith in God, I would continue to brave the odds and toil like my parents toiled before me.

I was proud of my immigrant roots. I was proud to contribute in my own small way to the country's development and progress. I was proud to be a part of the nation's backbone. With or without recognition, it will be the immigrant spirit that would continue to empower me to keep on making a difference. It was a blessing to be given an avenue to fulfill my dreams. It was an honor to be able to give back and pay it forward.

The immigrants who came before me, many years ago, led a very hard life. For them, it was survival of the fittest. Today, in one way or another, the challenges are still the same. But with some of the positive changes that have been made in contemporary times, we are facing less obstacles. There are more opportunities available in all sectors and levels. We scoured for jobs in a levelled playing field. We had overcome challenges and survived. We made good in our respective fields. We walked the streets of America with dignity, fulfillment, and gratitude in our journey of love, family, dreams, purpose, labor, sacrifice, self-discovery, and life.

CHAPTER 8
FAMILY

M y parents lived a simple life. They enjoyed simple pleasures while savoring the fruits of their labor. They were homebodies who loved to relax at home, at their own pace, and spend time all to themselves.

At home, they enjoyed watching TV, specially shows like *Family Feud*, *The Lawrence Welk Show*, *Good Morning America*, *The Price Is Right*, *American Ninja Warriors*, and shows and newscasts on Filipino channels. Dad also enjoyed watching action movies and sports like boxing, wrestling, mixed martial arts, UFC, NBA games, and the Olympics. They loved to listen to praise and gospel songs and Filipino, American and European classics. They would also croon over the songs of the Carpenters, Burt Bacharach. Andrea Bocelli, André Rieu, Josh Groban, Lawrence Welk, Elvis Presley, Anne Murray, Platters, Andy Williams, Paul Anka, Engelbert Humperdinck, Tom Jones and Filipino artists like Jose Mari Chan. Dad also would hit it with bouncy styles like the cha-cha and the mambo and even marching bands. When Dad and Mom would go out, their main activity was eating out at their favorite restaurants and sometimes watching movies at the theaters.

My parents never asked me to help shoulder expenses at home. They never asked for anything in return but appreciated little things that I did for them like when I treated them out or brought some goodies home. They were always grateful, but also ready to remind me not to spend too much on them and save instead for my family.

Their homesickness and longing to be with the family were constant. They enjoyed connecting with their grandchildren as the family grew with time. Some of their grandchildren had married and started their own families. They now had a growing number of great-grandchildren.

My parents would talk to their grandchildren about their lives, love life, studies, dreams, health, problems, and just about everything else. They were updated on who would marry next, who would graduate next semester, or who was celebrating a birthday that month. They would also call their grandchildren who worked overseas to see how they were doing. They would smile with glee as they looked at their great-grandchildren in photos and videos.

My parents were very proud and happy about their children and grandchildren's achievements no matter how big or small. They were very supportive, and prayed for our success. Dad would always raise the roof for our accomplishments. Even if we told him not to tell anyone about our achievements, he would still tell every Tom, Dick and Harry he met about them. It was not because he was boastful or a tell-all. It was because he was extremely happy for and proud of us. The next day, we would find ourselves being congratulated or praised by people we bumped into outside the house.

Dad and Mom looked at their nephews and nieces like their own children as they gave great importance to kinship. They prayed for and took pride in their achievements and successes in life. When Dad's nephew was elected mayor of a city in Santa Clara County in Silicon Valley, my parents were exhilarated. They excitedly prepared to attend their nephew's inaugural ceremony, even if it meant discomfort or difficulty because they had to travel. They were grateful that they had other nephews and nieces who were willing to pick them up and drive them home for every occasion. When another nephew was elected mayor in the town of Mangatarem, in the Philippines, they were as proud and happy as they were to any of their nephews and nieces in their endeavors, whether those were big or small.

Being family-oriented and clannish, Dad loved to video call his nephews, nieces, siblings, cousins, and friends from all parts of the world to update and reconnect with them. They would talk about the good old days. He would recall the jaunts and parties with his cousins, and those times he and his friends would go swimming in the river or at the beach. He would recall those big gatherings with family and relatives and trips to the bowling alleys with his nephews and nieces and hunting trips with his nephews in the mountains of Mangatarem. He was fond of sharing those stories to us. He reached out to both his side of the family and Mom's. Even during the times when he already had a hard time hearing and understanding what they told him, he would call everyone to see how they were doing.

Relatives and friends would visit my parents when they had the chance. Mom's former students and faculty members had come to visit. There was one batch who awarded Mom with a plaque of appreciation and another batch who gave Mom a huge, folded card with short messages from her former students who were working from here and afar. We had the card, which looked like a poster, framed and mounted on the wall. My mother's classmates from the Dominican-ran University of Santo Tomas College of Nursing in Manila who had migrated to the U.S., came for a visit. Mom would excitedly share nice stories of her former students, faculty and classmates with us. She had always been happy and proud of what they had achieved in life. Family and friends as well came for a visit from the U.S., the Philippines, and other countries. Mom's friends and fellow teachers from the university who could not travel, kept in touch through the telephone.

Those reunions sometimes became emotional and evoked nostalgic sentiments. Dad and Mom would always look forward to them as it gave them the opportunity to reconnect and cherish unforgettable memories. As my parents grew older, they had difficulty taking long trips. They could not visit relatives and friends. They usually could not attend weddings, funerals, and other events. They could only do so if their nephews and nieces drove them to and from their destination. As aging parents, they appreciated those visits. They were always grateful for those who would remember to call or visit them since they valued kinship and friendship.

Dad and Mom never tired of showering me with advice that comes with a sprinkling of adages and proverbs. I told them those were cliches and I had heard them many times before. When I was in a jocose mood, I would make fun of those phrases. They knew they had to put up with me even though my pranks and jokes were stale. Mom would tell me that even if they were hackneyed phrases, they were powerful words of wisdom that could help and guide people to face the trials and tribulations in life.

Mom would tell me to treat people the way I would like people to treat me. "Do not do unto others what you do not want others to do unto you." Mom told me to put the gist of this golden rule into my heart. She added that I should be kind to people and before I could get the love and respect of other people, I would have to first show my love and respect for them.

"If someone throws a stone at you, throw him a piece of bread." I told Mom I knew that proverb but that many people did not follow that in actual life. Mom said that was a pity. She believed that we needed compassion, understanding and patience to be able to do that. To enliven the serious mood, she tried to rib me with, "Don't tell me you would just throw back the bread but you have to place it in a jar." Mom jokingly forewarned me that she heard that answer many times from me. I had to change my tack with a rehashed answer. "No, Mom. I would only throw back the jar. I would eat the bread. I was hungry." At least it preempted Mom's anticipation.

Dad told me to wake up early so I could accomplish many things every day. He presented his own platitudes. "The early bird catches the worm."

I answered him with, "No, Dad. There's traffic. The bird was late. The worm had already gone."

Dad was frugal and knew how to manage his money. He had savings put safely aside and never faltered in paying the monthly bills. He would always advise me to save for the rainy days and for the future. I followed in Dad's footsteps when it comes to wise spending and saving money. One of my father's favorite phrases was, "A penny saved is a penny earned." I would tell Dad that a penny cannot buy anything. He would answer me that every penny counts. He was eager to tell me that if I saved a hundred pennies, that was equivalent to one dollar. I agreed that every cent would tote up, but I was tempted to add to and rephrase the quotation. "Ten bucks saved is ten bucks earned for a Mc-Donald's burger and fries." Dad sneered and mocked at my brand of corny jokes. My parents, however, knew in their hearts that I valued whatever lessons I got from their inspirational advice and quotations.

I was the most exuberant whenever Trina and Ken came to visit me in the U.S. I always looked forward to seeing them. Twice I ran short of cash to purchase their plane tickets, but when it came to my parents' attention, they purchased the tickets for me without me asking them. It was a gesture from them that I will always be indebted to them for.

The insurmountable challenges of long-distance relationships were intimidating. Trina and I tried to do whatever we could to make our relationship survive. We were working on the premise that we were both stakeholders and that what we were doing was for the family's future. Still, there were times when we could not help but argue about our situation. We vacillated on several issues that bugged us.

"Did I make the right decision to work in the U.S?"

"Shall I abandon my dreams and go back to my family in the Philippines?"

"Where will this pursuit lead us?"

"Is our long-distance relationship putting a dent in our marriage?"

I asked myself, "Why am I doing this? Why do I have to work in the U.S. away from my family?" My answer would always go back to the family.

It was the same reason why Trina and I were working so hard and looking for opportunities to give our son a good life. The difference was that I worked far away from home. It helped that our love for each other gave us strength that enabled us to face challenges and bear sacrifices and hardships. The sad thing was the distance would always break our hearts no matter how much we understood or prepared ourselves for the repercussions it entailed. It would leave pain and fear somewhere that lingered. Trina and Ken had come to visit me in the U.S. many times, but it was not enough to make up for the loneliness that we felt through the years.

It was hard that every year, I was not home to celebrate Christmas and New Year with them. It was hard that when Trina had a hysterectomy, I was not there to take care of her. It was hard that when she had a car accident, I was not there at her side to help and support her.

When I bought Ken a large battery-operated toy car in the U.S., he loved to play with it in the nearby Todos Santos Plaza. While he enjoyed playing with the car, I would sing a melody that I had taken from a TV car commercial. I would sing its simple lyrics "Zoom, Zoom, Zoom." When he and my wife returned to the Philippines, we had one phone conversation where Ken had questions about why I have not gone home yet with them. It was our fault, me and my wife, for not telling him the reason why I was in the U.S. I had to explain to my son, who was by then eight or nine years old, that I was working in the U.S. to give him a good future. I wanted to tell him how much I missed him. Holding my tears, I found myself belting out, "Zoom, Zoom, Zoom." Ken reacted to it. As I held my phone to my ear, I heard him crying like it poured after holding it back for some time. It was a cry coming from a small innocent boy who was trying to comprehend the missing pieces of his family life, especially the separation, the distance, and the sudden absence of each other in our lives. It was then that I understood why he was asking why I was far away from them. My son missed me so much. I felt the pain that had cut deeply in the long time that we had been separated from each other across the ocean.

As part of the equation with me, my wife did her part in pursuing our dreams for the family. She worked into a sales and marketing career and started a small business. But even with her busy schedule, she was always there to take care of our son. I felt bad that I could not do the same for our son. While Ken was growing up, it was hard that when he celebrated his birthdays and graduated from elementary and high school, I was not there to greet and hug him. It was hard that when he performed as the lead vocalist in the high school band, I was not there to watch him. It was hard that when he played as captain of the varsity basketball team, I was not there to support and cheer for him. It was hard for me. It was hard for Trina and Ken.

Because of the physical separation of the family, I missed a lot of Ken's growing up years. In the latter years of their U.S. visits, I was surprised to see that Ken was taller than me, with a deep voice and developing muscles. I knew him as a child, not as a young man. I used to play with him and carry him on my back or shoulders. One time I told him that I longed to carry him on my back like I used to do when he was a child. He laughed at me awkwardly, knowing that he was taller and quite heavier than me. He had no idea that I missed those happy and innocent times.

Now that he had grown up, his interests and activities had changed. He developed a passion for real cars and driving. I would pester him that he was spending more time with basketball and his band than his studies. He took after my father for being friendly, but I would remind him to only stay with friends who were good in their hearts and deeds. One time he had a quarrel with his girlfriend. I had to advise him because he was too young to fully understand the intricacies of love and relationships. I could not help but still look at my son as a child, despite the mature relationship that we had evolved into. It showed the gap in the years between us that we both missed.

When Trina and Ken were back in the Philippines, we connected on video calls. Having the benefits of free online communication platforms like Facetime and Messenger, we would spend time smiling and laughing and sharing endless stories through our cell phones. After those jovial calls, the sadness and tears would roll down our cheeks. We bore the pain by ourselves in silence.

As a young man with a wife and son, the family was still at the top of my priorities. As a young man with a dream, I could not give it all up just like that. My dreams were for my family. I felt that if I did not even try to pursue my dreams for my family, I was doing a disservice to them. Through the years, I had steadily gained headway in my endeavors toward the path of my dreams. Maybe Trina and I needed to give ourselves a little more time. Maybe more patience and sacrifices. Maybe more understanding for each other. With some more time and prayers, before we knew it, we would be where I had wanted my family to be.

Through the years of longing for my family, I spent my time at work as my outlet. On rare occasions, I would sit down to write. I wrote a poem for my son that was included in an anthology of poetry published in the U.S. I dedicated it to both my wife and son.

To My Son On His Journey

When I look back at the road I've passed
At times I thought I would not last
But each turn I took to the Lord I trust
Would lead me to my destiny at last
I've passed many crossroads along the way
I've taken wrong paths and lost my way
But faith has given me strength to find my way
And dignity that I was able to do it my way
When the road is rough, I comfort myself with a song
And sometimes, I have to rest when the road is long
But hardships and failures are just part of it all
What matters is what you had become after all
As you take your own road, this I shall say
Be brave, be strong and seize the day
Walk on the right path, never give up and always pray
For even when you're lost and weary
The Lord will be there to show the way

CHAPTER 9
FRICTION

Just like any other family, we were not without misunderstandings and conflicts. I was the stubborn kid in a brood of three brothers and one sister. When my siblings and I were small, we engaged in fistfights with each other over petty matters. My sister was not involved in any of our scuffles but most of the time, she became the target of our pranks and teasing. Sometimes we would go too far while teasing her. We would catch her in a corner sobbing.

Since *Kuya* Steve was the eldest, he would look after us in school and at home. When Mom was at work, he would help bathe us, prepare dinner, and put us to bed. He was protective of and concerned about his siblings. He had a passion for food and cooking. He and my mother were the ones who influenced me and created my passion for cooking. My siblings and I looked up to him with the kind of love and respect accorded to someone who is regarded as the second in command after my parents. Despite my love and respect for my brother, I rarely followed his instructions and stuck to my own opinions. Because of my hardheadedness, I locked horns with him. I got reprimanded by him, and sometimes took a whip from him.

Kuya James was my childhood playmate. We had many adventures and misadventures together. We did a lot of crazy things and kid stuff. He was the one I had fistfights with many times. Surprisingly, our quarrels led us to being closer to each other as we grew up. He loved to eat but he was not that keen to work in the kitchen. He grew more heavier than all of us in time. When Chloe was born, *Kuya* James and I took turns taking care of her when Mom was at work. By that time, *Kuya* Steve was already staying with my grandmother in Manila to attend college.

Because of our mischief, *Kuya* James and I drew Dad's ire. If we misbehaved too much, my father would crack the whip to discipline us. We would get bouts of jitters when we knew we had disobeyed his mandate and Dad was mad. When Dad scolded us, we would be quiet and meek as lambs as we listened to his scolding. Since I had always been outspoken, sometimes I would answer him back. As expected, I always ended up getting the belt smacked on my butt.

Dad and I would always be the ones getting into misunderstandings. If we had arguments, I would speak my mind and unwittingly answer him back. It would naturally hit my father's raw nerve. That was during my younger and unfiltered days. I now realize how hard it was for him to control us and balance his disciplinary actions toward his kids. The good thing was my parents somehow treated us equally and fairly as we grew up.

As parents, they would forgive us for our misdeeds. My parents' forgiveness eclipsed our sibling quarrels. My brothers and I would settle our differences. We would discover that despite our differences, we were somehow the same after all. We would understand each other without having the need to explain ourselves thoroughly. We would rediscover the love and bond that we had for each other. Dad and Mom would clamp the lid down on the family and bring back the laughter and joy that we had in our happy home. Dad was more of a disciplinarian than Mom was. When I was in high school in the Philippines, he made it clear to his children that he did not want to see us drinking and smoking. When he was our age, those were his vices. Although he was not an addict or alcoholic, his vices got him into fights and some trouble. He did not want us to be like him. He did not want to see us get involved in brawls. He wanted to protect us. He drew us away from a path that would lead us to a wasted life of addiction and alcoholism. He wanted us to do well in our studies and focus on making our lives better.

Unbeknownst to Dad, I tried drinking and smoking in school to be accepted in a clique. Since it was the "in" thing to do, I was egged on through peer pressure to try them. One night I told Dad I was going to a birthday party. I was actually going to a newly opened bar downtown. My classmate asked me if I would go with him. I accepted the invite but at the last minute, he cancelled because of a headache. Since I was already at the downtown venue, I decided to go into the new bar by myself. As a start, I ordered a bottle of beer.

I told *Kuya* James where I was really going. He felt uneasy that I had lied to Dad about the birthday party. Out of concern for my safety, he told Dad where I was really headed to. My father hopped from one bar to another to track me down. Out of the blue, I spotted him entering the bar. He scolded me and reprimanded the manager and the waitstaff for serving beer to a minor. Before we left, he warned the manager that he would have the whole place padlocked to give them a lesson.

For two weeks, I was grounded. It was better than being

padlocked. What mattered was that I had learned my lesson well. After that, I learned to respect my parents' protective instincts, guiding principles, and concern for their children. I saw for myself how my father would face anyone, and anything, and all dangers and obstacles, to protect me. I had firmly decided never to touch alcohol or cigarettes again. My two brothers, who hung out with various group of friends, did smoke and drink in their adulthood but only during occasional social gatherings. I remember seeing them smoke and drink only a few times, and not before my father. They understood their limitations and responsibilities, and my father's rule.

As I grew into adulthood and maturity, my conflict with *Kuya* Steve and my father had considerably lessened. This time, if we would have arguments, it would be more of a mature exchange of opinions. There were a few times when it would end up in a heated exchange of words. We would have disagreements because we always had conflicting ideas and beliefs. After our heated exchanges, we would always feel sorry about our outbursts. We would realize that we were still the same family that we all belong to and were a big part of. Despite our egos and pride, and despite our differences in our viewpoints, it was never too late to remember that we loved each other after all.

When I lived with my parents in the U.S., what usually caused a certain amount of friction between Dad and me was the remittances he sent to the Philippines. My parents sent regular payments to help support my siblings in the Philippines. There is nothing wrong with helping the family when they are in need. It was normal for Filipinos who were based abroad to send money back home. What I was concerned about was my parents' own welfare and financial security. Whenever I asked about their remittance, Dad would often misinterpret it as a refusal on my part to help my siblings. It was not the case.

"Do not be miserly with your siblings," Dad would tell me with conviction. "If they need help, let us help them. You cannot play deaf or look the other way."

I would explain that I was thinking about *their* well-being. I did not want to see him scrimp on some things he needed so he could save more money to send home.

He would expound back, "I worked hard and sacrificed a lot for all of you. On their own, your siblings have been trying hard enough to earn their keep. Their salaries are not enough to make ends meet. I would do the same to help you if you were in the same situation."

"I know about that, Dad," I would retort back. "I also ask for your help like my siblings do. I love my siblings and I want them to have a good life. I just want to see them stand on their own feet more so they can find their own path to success."

Dad would stick to his stand. "We cannot ignore your siblings' plight. There's no one else who can help them. I don't want anyone in the family to be deprived."

I would also stick to my stand. "All I am saying is do not overdo it. You might be doing more harm than good."

Dad would start getting annoyed. "If you don't want to help, then don't. I am not asking you to help. But if your siblings need help, Mommy and I will always be ready to bail them out," Dad would say with finality.

I would still butt in with, "Dad, you and Mom are old. What you need to do is stop working and enjoy life. That's what you deserve."

"No," he would answer back. "Your siblings still need

our support. That's why we're working."

"Dad, I'm willing to do my share. But if I'm going to help my siblings, I want to help them learn to help themselves because I want to see them make it on their own," I would answer back.

"Your siblings have been striving hard. They have been doing their best. They have been overcoming hardships. Someday they will achieve their dreams and have a better life too," Dad assured me.

I would reply with, "I want the same thing for my siblings. But what I'm telling you to do is to balance everything when you help them. I don't care if you send a large or small amount, or if you send it once or twice a month. The important thing is how it will really help them in the short and the long term."

"Can't you see that's what I'm doing?" Dad would ask.

"Yes, Dad," I would quickly reply. "But make sure you weigh everything at hand. Next time you sent money, make sure it's worth sending them and see how it can benefit them the most."

"Times have been hard," Dad butted in. "Our help means so much to them. They are our family. We are better off here than they are there. Why can't we share what we are blessed to have here?"

"Dad, you must know how to see the difference between charity and dole outs. Also, try to see how we can make the money you send to them grow," I intimated.

Dad would sigh to hint that our argument was going around in circles or was going nowhere. "When your son grows up and asks for your help, you will understand what I feel as a father who wants to be there at all times to support his children who are struggling in life."

I would tell Dad that I truly understood his stand as much as I understood why my siblings were asking for their help.

"I understand that my sibling's plight compelled them to seek your help. I know that once they have a better income, they will not be asking for your help anymore and it will be time for them to give back. My point is that when you help them, don't let them get used to it or depend on it. Otherwise, they will not be motivated to do their best.

Dad would present his position. "That's my point. Your siblings need help right now so we are helping them. Once they start earning enough, they should be able to stand on their own. They have always been trying to give their best shot in life. Should we not give them the support they need when we can? It's that simple."

During our heated arguments, Mom would step in to neutralize and calm us down. Exhausted from it all, Dad would stand up and retreat to his room.

In the end, we would totally understand each other. We would realize that both of us wanted to be there for the family. I understood Dad's father side of the argument. He loved his family so much that he could not deny them. I knew that it was his money that he was sending and that he was accountable for his own money. It was for him to decide what he would like to do with his money. I could only make suggestions.

On my father's side, I know that he was listening to what I was telling him. He knew that I was as concerned about my siblings as he was. He was just trying to be as fair as possible and dependable for help to his children. He wanted to be a strong pillar to the family. Our common denominator was to help in the family. We just had different approaches.

We were divided by generational mindsets and beliefs. We ignored the fact that we only need to understand each other and meet halfway. We did not have to be at each other's throats. Our arguments should not break us apart.

I knew what life was like in the Philippines. The Philippine economy was getting better but economic opportunities were still limited. My brother Steve was a computer programming and medical technology graduate but preferred to venture into business. His business was doing well, but it went through ups and downs. My brother James was an architecture graduate. He worked at a construction company in Manila, but his salary was not enough to make ends meet.

I knew that if my brothers did not need it, they would not ask for help from my parents. Their circumstances necessitated certain actions that they needed to do for their families. I could have been in the same situation as my brothers in the Philippines. If my salary were not enough to make both ends meet, I would be forced to ask for help from my parents. Even if I did not want to do that, I would be forced to do it if it meant survival for my family.

Dad had strong convictions about his beliefs and principles. He was tough and never cowered in a fight, except in fights with Mom. He would give in to Mom when she started to cry. Mom was the type who would rather yield or not comment at all so as not to hurt other people's feelings. However, when it came to defending or fighting for her children, she was a frontliner.

If Mom was the reserved, homebody type, Dad was the extrovert type. Dad easily made friends. He made friends with everyone, whether they were white, black, yellow, brown, or let us say young or old, or rich or poor. He had no racial or social prejudices. When his neighborhood friends saw him on the porch, they would approach him to engage in conversations.

My parents would go out of their way to extend a help-ing hand to neighbors in need. One day, a neighbor-friend called at 4 a.m. to ask for help when he found out his ailing wife had died in her sleep. Dad and Mom immediately got dressed and went over to see our neighbor who was too shocked and perplexed to be able to do anything at all at that moment. They called his daughter who lived in the next city and then called 911 while staying there with their neigh-bor to comfort him.

We had a widowed neighbor-friend who banged on the door one night. She needed help and asked to be taken to the hospital. Her speech was slurred, and she almost col-lapsed on the floor. We helped her over to the sofa and im-mediately called 911. She was taken to the hospital where she received immediate medical attention. She had a stroke. Our neighbor-friend survived her ordeal and recovered.

My parents took to the habit of reading the Bible and praying every day. They took their church obligations and assigned tasks at Holy Mass to heart. My parents' devotion to their faith rubbed off on us as me and my siblings grew up to be God-fearing Catholics and practiced our Catholic education in our daily lives.

After Queen of All Saints Church, my parents became parishioners at St. Francis of Assisi Church, also in Concord. Every Saturday afternoon, they attended the Anticipatory Mass where they served as offerers. Their simple role in the Mass was to bring the sacramental wine and hosts for the sacrament of Holy Communion to the officiating priest who was waiting at the altar. They did that during Saturday Mass for many years.

When I hosted a nine-day novena to Our Lady of Manaoag, I depended on my parents to take care of inviting people, buying and serving refreshments, and leading the daily novena prayers. I could not take care of the novena myself because of all the work. Dad and Mom successfully conducted the novena activities. On the last day, I was able to attend the novena prayers. We invited a priest to celebrate Mass and we prepared food for the attendees.

Through the years, I also saw Dad's effort to fulfill his commitment to our altar at home. His commitment was to buy a bunch of roses every week and place it at the altar. When Dad passed, my sister Chloe picked up where Dad left off. She took the initiative to make sure that the altar had fresh flowers every week and has continued that up to this day.

During the times I was looking for a job, Dad persuaded me to practice driving. The first time I took the steering wheel, he got tense whenever I committed the slightest mistake. He sat in the passenger seat next to me to give me instructions.

"Step on the break!"

"Slow down here!"

"Look at the side mirror!"

I told him, "Dad, I drive in the Philippines. Let me be."

"No," he protested. "It's different here. They're much stricter here with traffic rules and cops are always around watching!"

I said, "I know, Dad, but don't be frantic. You're confusing me more than teaching me."

"Reduce the speed and step on the break!" he frantically told me as if I did not know that was what I should be doing.

"I know, Dad. It's a yellow light," I replied.

"Always be careful. You have to wait for the green light," Dad butted in, but I did not react. Sometimes it was better not to answer back. Dad continued talking. "When you are driving, always take precautions and be alert." The traffic light had turned green, and I had not moved. The car behind us blew its horn impatiently. "Go, go, go!" Dad prodded me impatiently. "What do you think you're doing, son?"

Before we started getting more on each other's nerves, I asked Dad to take the wheel and drive us home, lest we end up crashing into a light pole. I knew Dad wanted me to practice driving safely. He had good intentions. He was just overly concerned and agitated by my little mistakes. While he was driving home, he was quiet and relaxed. He had loosened up from the tension. We made it home safely with no arguments and with our sanity intact.

There was one time I sneaked out Dad's car from the common parking area to drive to the stores downtown. I timed it when my father was taking a nap in the afternoon. I knew how long he slept. We live in the heart of downtown so going to the store is just about 2 to 3 minutes' drive away. I drove back home in time, fast enough not to be caught, before Dad woke up. He would have fumed if he found out. That would have been a safety and security breach to him. It was a violation of traffic laws. I did not have a driver's license. That was the reason why Dad did not want me to drive by myself or buy me a car.

One day, a neighbor told Dad that he saw me driving a few days ago and would like to hitch a ride next time if I would be going to the grocery store. Dad was upset and reprimanded me why I sneaked out the car. He enumerated the violations that I did, the penalty and court fine that I could face and the consequences of my misbehavior. I doffed my hat to my father for knowing and abiding by the law. He warned me not to do it again. Of course, I never got the chance to sneak out the car again because I never got to see where he kept his car key in the house after that.

CHAPTER 10

IMMIGRATION

The comprehensive immigration reform program proposed by President Barack Obama stalled in Congress. Demoralized for still being in the shadows, Mom would tell me to keep praying and holding on for solutions. Dad would assure me that we will continue looking for ways to change my status. "It's okay, son. We can look for other legal steps. Let's wait awhile."

My parents never wanted me to be a TNT (short for *tago ng tago,* which is a term used by Filipinos that refers to undocumented people, and particularly to fellow Filipinos). They prodded me to consult with some immigration lawyers to see if there were still options to change my papers. They all proposed that I wait for my petition's priority date to become current, so I could apply for an adjustment of status. My petition's priority date would take many more years to become current. If that was the only possible step that I could take, I had no choice but to wait.

Immigration had become a subject of intense debate, polarizing the viewpoints of Americans. Even in the circle of family and friends, there would be those who favored and those who did not favor immigration reforms, especially when it comes to granting legal residency to undocumented immigrants.

My parents became interested in immigration issues

because of my status. Dad watched the news on TV and updated me with anything he heard about immigration. Mom clipped relevant newspaper articles for my reference file.

During President Donald Trump's term, my chances to resolve my immigration problem became more adverse. His framework on immigration reform provided a very limited platform to legalize the status of illegal immigrants. He issued executive orders to enforce restrictions on immigration. So now even more, my case stagnated. I had to have a lot of patience to wait for any development in immigration.

Fortunately, fast forward to February 2021, my priority date became current. That meant I could start the process of applying to adjust my status and eventually get my green card. Chloe had arrived as an immigrant in 2016 through the same petition that me and my brothers had from my mom. Her petition moved faster because she was single, although she still waited for a long time. When she arrived, she was already in her thirties and had worked as a radio disc jockey and call center supervisor in the Philippines.

My parents and two brothers had since passed without seeing the realization of our dreams to be together in the United States. Now that they were gone, I was even more determined to get my papers fixed in honor of their memory and for my own family. In the afterlife, I knew they would be happy for me and would achieve their realizations through me.

Through the protracted years that I was looking for immigration solutions, I also saw my parents advance with age and become sickly. Dad had medical issues normal for an aging person like diabetes, high blood pressure, and arthritis. Otherwise, he was in good physical condition. Mom was frail and she would get sick often. We would rush her to the emergency room, sometimes in the wee hours of the morning or late at night. It helped that the hospital was just a few minutes' drive from the apartment.

It bothered me that if the full extent of immigration laws were executed for undocumented people like me, I might be deported back to the Philippines. I worried about my parents. It was hard to leave them alone, given their age and medical conditions. That was one reason why I seriously wanted to fix my immigration papers. Besides, it had been years since I had been away from my wife and son. I had wished that my wife and son could live with us in the U. S. legally so we could look after each other and take care of Dad and Mom. In that case, I would not have to divide my worries between my family in the Philippines and my parents in the U.S.

There was a time when Dad was confined at the John Muir Medical Center in Walnut Creek for hypertension and respiratory ailment. It so happened that at the same time, Mom was not feeling well. That happened about two years before Chloe had arrived in the U.S. I had to divide my time between taking care of Dad in the hospital, and my sick mother at home. I would wake up early to cook Mom's food for the day before I headed to the hospital in Walnut Creek. I would stay with Dad for some time to attend to his needs, and then leave him in the afternoon. I would be home by early evening to prepare dinner for Mom. I followed that routine for five days. My mother would often cry because she worried both about my father's condition and my situation, and she could not do anything to help. I assured her that everything was going to be alright, and all she needed to do was rest and get well herself.

There was another time Dad woke me up at 4 a.m. to take

Mom to the hospital. She had diarrhea and was vomiting. Mom and I waited in the living room while Dad went to get his car. When he came back, he was frantic. Our car and three other cars parked side by side next to our car in the common parking area had been broken into. The windows in all the four cars were smashed. Our car's front windows on the driver and passenger sides were busted.

We never left anything of value in our car. Still, the robbers took every little thing we had in the car like a ballpoint pen, a handy notepad, a small flashlight, and a small box of tissues among other things. I had to call a taxi to take Mom to the hospital. Dad had to stay behind to wake up the neighbors and call the police. Our neighbors thought that more than one person may have carried out the auto burglaries.

Those incidents attested to the need for someone who could look after and respond to my parents during emergencies or when something came up. It bolstered the importance of having me living with them so I could help them out. There was nobody else they could rely on at any time or in any situation. That said, I had an American coworker who look at it otherwise. When he learned that I lived with my parents, he nudged me to get a life while I am young. "Why the hell do you live with your parents? C'mon man. Get a life!"

My coworker's unsolicited advice was well-meaning. He was encouraging me to strike while the iron was hot and have fun and adventure in my life on my own. I thought his outlook on life was influenced by culture and lifestyles. That thought enabled me to look at sociological angles about how people conducted their lives based on their culture, beliefs, needs, and environment.

I was told that for Americans, once you reach the age of eighteen, you are allowed to leave home and be on your own to start building your life. For Filipinos, no matter if you are an adult who is working or not, single, or married with children, it is normal to live with your parents. Or the parents can live with their children, whether their children are single or married and with a family. Probably what really worked depended on the individual, the family, their current situation, and what worked or was convenient for them.

As for me, I was good living with my parents. I was beholden to them. I was demonstrating my filial piety to them. I was done with getting a life when I was younger. I was having a life with my parents. My Mom, in her motherly desire to see her children get the best out of their lives, told me that I could choose to live with them or on my own. It all depended on the lifestyle that I want to achieve, the circumstances and what suits my needs. She told me that either way is good as long as I am able to enjoy and make the most out of my life and explore all possibilities and opportunities to achieve my dream while I am young and able.

CHAPTER 11
REMINISCENCES

R eminiscing about the days with my parents spoke volumes of memories to share. Those memories were trivial to me when they were alive, but when they passed away, those memories became my bridge to the wonderful life that we shared together. When I thought about them, I would recall memories that transformed into something as alive and vibrant as the beat that pulsated in my heart.

Christmas was the most important holiday in the family, followed by New Year's. In the U.S., the three of us had adopted Thanksgiving to celebrate too. Our celebrations highlighted food and family togetherness, complemented by gift-giving and holiday decorations. Christmas was centered on the religious belief that Jesus Christ was born to spread the good tidings of love, hope, peace, and joy to mankind. Following religious traditions, when Dad and Mom were still able, they attended the nine-day *Simbang Gabi* (the Filipino Christmas Novena Dawn Masses) at St. Francis of Assisi Church in Walnut Creek. Most of the time we attended the Masses with some of our Filipino neighbors. They practiced this tradition every year, even when they had to go to work afterwards. They enjoyed eating *Puto Bumbong* and *Bibingka* (native rice cakes), and other breakfast stuff provided free by the Filipino community.

As Mom got older, she found it hard and tiring to cook food in bulk for the holidays. Dad had to order our holiday food from restaurants and friends. The three of us would go from one place to another to pick up the food he had ordered. He would order *Egado* (an Ilokano dish of pork loin meat with pork liver and other innards cooked in soy sauce and vinegar], *Morcon* (a Filipino meat roll], *Lengua* (beef tongue stew), and a huge Honey-Baked Ham. To supplement the ordered food, Mom would make whatever was easy for her to cook like *Kaldereta* (a tomato-based beef stew cooked with liver spread, potatoes and carrots) or *Pochero* [beef or pork belly stew cooked in tomato sauce with *saba* banana, cabbage and long green beans). She would always make potato salad and fruit salad for dessert.

The taste and smell of the food reminded me of the holidays in the Philippines. It reminded me of the gastronomes in us, and our enthusiasm for life that was celebrated with food to bring the family together. It might help to understand that Mom's roots traced back to Pampanga, a province in Central Luzon, which is known as the Culinary Capital of the Philippines.

My mother's side of the family were ardent foodies in their own right. I have cousins who were adventurous and daring enough to juggle exploring the most exotic street food with eating at classy and expensive restaurants at any place in the world they might happen to be in. My grandmother, whom we address us Nanay [mother], honed her culinary skills from what was passed on to her in the family. That was one reason why she cooked the best homegrown style *Lumpiang Sariwa* (fresh lumpia or fresh eggroll), *Pancit Palabok* (Filipino noodles), *Adobo* (chicken or pork or both cooked in soy sauce and vinegar), *Morcon* (Filipino meat roll), *Kare- Kare* [oxtail stew with vegetable and rich peanut sauce], and other Filipino favorites. Nanay was a teacher who raised her four children all by herself when my grandfather died at a young age. My Mom, who was the eldest of her children, was only seven years old then. Nanay never remarried and focused her life in providing for her children who all became accomplished professionals.

On my father's side, my *Lola* (grandmother) was always at the helm to prepare for big feasts. When the fiesta (town feast) or Lola's birthday approached, she would ask Dad to summon their favorite local cook. My grandmother, along with Dad and the cook, would meet to plan the menu and budget for the dishes and other preparations, including the cook and his team's emolument.

The cook would suggest delectable dishes and delicacies that he knew my grandmother's guests would love. The agreement would be a package deal where the cook took care of everything, including purchasing and marketing, preparing, cooking, and cleaning up after the fiesta. The cook would buy the best live swine and poultry, the best cut of beef, the freshest fish and shrimp and a variety of the freshest vegetables, spices and herbs that he could find in the local market. His assistants and my grandmother's household helpers provided backup support. The cook and his assistants had to sleep over at my grandmother's house for a few days. They had to organize and accomplish their culinary tasks and commitments satisfactorily. With that, they were assured that my grandmother would summon them for the next feast.

Our fiesta celebrations before were festive with parades, shows, games and talent competitions. People always look forward to preparing for and attending them. In Dagupan

City, in the province of Pangasinan where I grew up, the fiesta is held on December 26-27, which is in-between Christmas and New Year celebrations. Many residents would arrange for their baptismal or wedding parties, class reunions or school homecoming and even birthday parties to coincide with the fiesta dates to celebrate double occasions in one celebration. You can imagine the nonstop partying and gift-giving in our city when this season comes. This is excluding company and school Christmas parties and get-together with friends and relatives. Invitations come on top of the other.

Holidays in the U.S. were always exciting, especially when the three of us would start putting up our medium-sized Christmas tree in the living room. Dad bought twinkling lights that we wrapped around the tree. Mom bought colorful ornaments that we hung all over the tree. We would leave a space beneath the Christmas tree for the *Belen* (nativity or manger tableau), and for our gifts.

In front of the apartment, I would help Dad install Christmas lights and hang the huge Filipino *parol* (Christmas lantern made from colorful capizes with dancing LED lights) on the porch. He ordered the *parol* through a commercial he saw on a Filipino TV channel. It reminded me of our family tradition in the Philippines where the family gathered to help put up a tall Christmas tree that almost reached the ceiling in the living room. Then, we would hang the parol and install Christmas lights in the garden in front of our house.

In the Philippines, we started preparing for Christmas as early as September. It was not unusual to see Christmas trees and decorations at businesses or private houses and hear Christmas carols starting on that month. While in the

U.S., an American neighbor was amazed by how early we were putting up our Christmas tree. We would usually put up our Christmas tree a few days before Thanksgiving Day in November. We imparted to her that Filipinos have the longest Christmas celebration that starts on the first of September and lasts until the Feast of the Three Kings in January. I also added that we have the merriest celebration of Christmas in the world.

There was a time when our apartment management sponsored a Christmas decoration contest for the tenants. They were going to pick the top three apartments with the most attractive presentations on their porches. Mom conceptualized a mini-Christmas playhouse theme that the three of us put together. We blended the decorations and dancing lights into a sparkling and colorful spectacle that adorned the porch. We assembled Mom's collection of large battery-operated moving Santa Clauses, Christmas ornaments, and displays, and placed them around the porch. Jolly Christmas carols that churned out from the ornaments and displays added an air of enchantment and merriment to the theme.

Our apartment was chosen as one of the top three winners in the contest. We received a small box of chocolates as our prize. It was a small reward, but it was a sweet symbol of the triumph of the Christmas spirit to us. Whether we had won or not, our real victory and happiness was seeing people smiling and cheering as they gazed at the winning "masterpiece" on our porch. Besides, the wonderful bonding the three of us enjoyed putting up the decorations enriched the Christmas spirit in our hearts.

Besides Christmas memories, I would remember those days when Dad would repeatedly call two to three times every night to check on me on my way home from the Concord BART station. He did that because he worried for my safety. I had to walk five blocks at night to get home. I was dumb not to answer his calls most of the time because I was always in a hurry. It did not matter to me that Dad was a worrier and that I was punishing him by not answering his calls. But the true father that he was, he never stopped calling me every night throughout the years that I lived with them, even though I repeatedly ignored his calls. Now that Dad is gone, I wish he had known how much I appreciated his care and concern that never wavered.

Dad and Mom would always wait for me to come home so we could have dinner together. If I told them I would be coming home late, they would not go to sleep until I got home. I told them they did not have to do that, but they would insist on waiting for me. I did not want them to eat dinner and sleep late because that would be bad for their health, but they would not listen to me. They were concerned about my safety. I would tell them in jest that I already felt like an upset father taking care of two hardheaded children in the house, referring to them. My parents would look at me and laugh heartily.

One time I went to San Francisco to shop for a gift and some other items. I also went to try a newly opened Italian restaurant in North Beach. I was supposed to be working that day but a coworker had exchanged his day off with me that week. I forgot to tell Dad and Mom about it.

Going back home, I had to catch the train before 9:30 p.m. from the Powell Street BART station. That schedule would bring me home to Concord at around 10:30 p.m., the usual time I arrive at home from work. But as fate would have it, the train was immobilized at the Powell Street station because of a technical glitch. I wanted to call Dad and Mom to tell them I would be home late because of the unscheduled train delay. But by coincidence, my phone battery went dead. I was unable to receive and make calls, leaving my parents clueless as to where I was and what was going on with me.

It took some time before the glitch was fixed. I was home shortly before midnight, safe and sound, and glad to see my parents relieved of their worrying. It was not the end of the story, though. Earlier that night, Dad had called me many times but was not able to reach me. Later into the night, Dad and Mom were already overwhelmed with anxiety. Dad called some of my friends to ask about my whereabouts. A few of them were already asleep when he called. Those friends called each other to ask about me. They all reached out to me, but no calls went through. At home, I had to call my friends back one by one, to tell them I just arrived home safe and apologize for the confusion and for disturbing them with our calls at such an ungodly hour. I was grateful that my friends were understanding and concern enough about me. It was an embarrassing moment, but it had shown me that my parents would do the unthinkable if they thought I was in peril.

One time I got complimentary tickets to an NBA game. Dad and I went to Oracle Arena in Oakland to watch a game between the Golden State Warriors and the L.A. Lakers. Before the game started, we tucked away burgers with fries and soda from one of the concessionaires. Dad and I had a grand time watching the exciting game together. Watching the NBA game live in person for the first time with my father was one of my most unforgettable moments with Dad.

When Dad and Mom still had the enthusiasm, physical

capability, and energy to go out to different places, I brought them to concerts, restaurants, and museums. I took them to choral concerts at the Cathedral of Christ the Light in Oakland. I bought them tickets to Filipino singer Martin Nievera's concert at the Concord Hilton. They enjoyed their jaunt to the California Academy of Sciences where they watched sharks and schools of colorful fish species in the huge aquarium. They also enjoyed the four-story living rainforest, planetarium, and natural history museum. Close by, they enjoyed horticultural wonders at the Japanese Tea Garden, the Conservatory of Flowers, and the San Francisco Botanical Garden. I also took them to good restaurants in San Francisco and Oakland whenever I get a longer time off from work.

Besides basketball, billiards, and cycling, Filipinos are big fans of boxing. Our greatest boxing hero is Manny Pacquiao. Filipinos would watch Pacquiao's pay-per-view boxing bouts in large groups or with families, which would include tables set with food like it was a party. It was the same for the three of us at home in the U.S. We watched every one of Manny Pacquiao's fights in collective exuberance with party food on the table.

To be able to watch Pacquiao's fights at home, I had to request time off from work. Then I would order food for the party for the three of us. As we watched, Dad would roar like a lion in the jungle while Mom was demure with her cheers in the corner. In the heat of the fight, Dad would alternately sit down and stand up as he watched the action in the boxing ring. If Pacquiao took a beating in one round, he would swear and sigh in dissatisfaction. If Pacquiao displayed dominance in another round, he would grit his teeth and clench and move his fist like he was punching

Pacquiao's opponent himself. He would yell out, "Knock him down!" like he was directly commanding Pacquiao in person to knock his opponent out. When Pacquiao would throw a powerful punch against his opponent, Dad and I would cheer and shout out loud in excitement, making Mom worried about the neighbors. If Pacquiao ultimately won the match, we would all be in a state of euphoria. Dad was the most jubilant. His triumphant blare reverberated victoriously inside the apartment.

There was a time when Dad and I confronted a rude taxi driver. Dad was asking for a receipt, but the driver did not want to issue one. When Dad insisted, it pissed the driver off. He finally issued the receipt but threw it at Dad. I yelled at the driver, "He's my father. What the hell are you doing?" I slammed the taxi door so it went with a bang. Dad did the same thing on the other door where he got off. I then yelled at the seemingly perplexed, pot-bellied driver, "Get lost." The driver hastily pulled away without uttering a word.

Dad and I also encountered an angry lady who accused us of taking her parking space without asking for her permission. After our car was broken into at the time we had to take Mom to the hospital, Dad looked for a gated parking area in the neighborhood where he could securely park his car. He found one nearby. The landlady happily gave us a parking space in her apartment building for $150 a month. But it turned out that the spot belonged to the angry lady who was the old landlady's tenant but who has yet to buy a car. The landlady had clandestinely rented out the parking space to us without us knowing that it belonged to a tenant. Apparently, the tenant was never informed about it too. In other words, we were both duped.

We were only able to use the parking slot overnight.

When we came the next morning to pick up our car, the tenant was already there waiting for us. She was understandably mad at us, but she was barking up the wrong tree. We tried to explain to her what had happened, but she did not care to listen or did not believe us. Our altercation escalated when she told us that we were stealing her parking space. She pointed her index finger at Dad and told him, "You get out of my parking slot, or I'll call the police right now and get you arrested." We tried our best to control our temper, but we lost it. We blew our tops and told her to go ahead and see who got into trouble for accusing us of a crime we never committed. We understand that we did not have the right to park on her parking slot and we were willing to go and give it back to her, but she had to understand herself that we were not to be blamed, neither she. We were both victims. We were both ripped off.

Dad called the landlady who answered with lack of interest. She reasoned out that she had been disturbed from her sleep. "Juancho, why did you wake me up for a measly $150? Let me go back to sleep." It was 11:45 a.m., almost lunchtime, when Dad called her. The landlady apparently wanted to rip us off our $150. It was hard to imagine that an old moneyed lady could be as cunning and deceptive that she could feign indifference so she could wash her hands of and find her way out of the mess she created. She even had the gull to counterplay Dad's conscience by making Dad look like he was bothering her for what she called a measly $150 that she did not want to return. I was sure the angry tenant had complained to her about the parking snafu, but I guess the tenant could have been shown the same indifference. When Dad called the landlady, it was not because he wanted his money back. It was to tell her that there was a confusion [Dad used the kindest term he could think of to avoid embarrassing the landlady] in the parking slot she gave us. I advised Dad to forget it and look for parking space elsewhere close to our apartment.

In 2014, I gave Mom a birthday party at her favorite Chinese restaurant. We invited about thirty guests and it was a memorable party for her. I did the same for Mom's birthday in 2015 at another restaurant. But in 2016, I had to cancel my reservation because Mom was sick. In the years that followed, the same thing happened because Mom was getting sick more often.

In 2014, Mom was turning eighty-three years old. I promised myself to give her a birthday party every year from then on. She was old and sickly. I wanted to give her something she would cherish. Deep inside, it was also my opportunity to repay her for my misdeeds of many years ago. It was a much-delayed payback, but at least I was able to do it for her.

Foremost in my idea of giving Mom a birthday party every year was to make her happy on her special day. I did not tell her about my underlying desire to redress the blunder I had made when she was a college dean in the Philippines. Otherwise, she would have told me not to worry about it and refused any offer of payback.

My blunder happened when Mom had a birthday celebration at her school many years ago. I told her I would pick up the tab for the catering. She declined but I insisted. During the party, she was so proud and happy to announce that her son was the one who was providing the food. She and her guests waited excitedly for a long time, but not a morsel of food arrived. Unknowingly, I had run short of money to be able to order food for the party. I had the impulse to recklessly abort my commitment without even bothering to inform Mom. She called, but I was too ashamed to answer, since I had no idea how and what to tell her. Perhaps I just did not have the guts to tell her. I did not know how to handle the imbroglio I created. Mom, of course, had to save face. She ordered food pronto for her hungry guests who did not deserve to be stood up by me.

When I came home that night, Mom was preparing her birthday dinner for the family. She warmly hugged me. It was like she was telling me that everything was okay, and that I was more important than any blunder that I committed. She only told me that I should have let her know there was a problem so she could have acted sooner. She never mentioned anything more about it to me or anyone in the family. I did not feel a tinge of hatred or anger from her. She owned and kept the humiliation all to herself. It was myopic and brainless of me that, back then, I never realized how I snafued my mother's birthday party and brought her to shame. I was too indifferent that I did not even apologize to her for my irresponsible and immature behavior.

While living in the U.S., Mom did not really want me to give her a birthday party because she wanted me to save my money for my family. But I was tenacious in my intention. It was my volition that I did it, to show my gratitude to my mother who had owned my blunder. She carried the pain in silence and forgave me without conditions. She positioned herself at the front to be a shock absorber and shield to save me from embarrassment. She knew I made an honest mistake that was why she did not give me tongue-lashing to make me feel wretched. Instead, she gave me a one-time reminder that I should have told her early so she could have addressed the problem sooner. I knew Mom was hurt the most in the incident, but she never showed it. She never scolded me to hurt me back for causing the mess. She gave me the time and chance to process, discern, recover, and rectify on my own the mess I had caused. I had learned my lesson and my blunder never happened again. Besides that, I became more careful with my words and actions because if I offended or did that to other people, my parents would be the first one to discipline me.

Throwing a birthday party for Mom was part of the realization to make my mother happy as I was happy for what I did for her. Of course, Dad shared our sentiments, but he forewarned me not to give him a birthday party because, just like mom, he would rather have it quietly at home with us. Seeing Mom happy somehow assuaged whatever guilt I had carried in my heart from my blunder.

Dad retired from his job at the hospital in 2013 at the age of eighty. He had worked there for fourteen years. Some concerned friends had encouraged him to retire a few years before that but he would not budge, knowing he still had the ability and energy to do his job. He just did not want to put that to waste. When he retired, he was still as healthy as a bull and was reluctant to slow down. His reflexes were good, but his hearing was impaired. He still had good eyesight, though, as he can still play crossword puzzle every day. He was so unrelenting to our advice for him to give up driving that he even bought a brand-new Honda Pilot in 2016 so he can drive Mom around in a more comfortable and updated car.

My father's parents and siblings lived long lives. An older sister of Dad's surpassed one hundred years old. Perhaps, genetics played a part in it. Also, my Lolo [grandfather] was a doctor who took care of the family's health.

My grandfather could have ingrained in the family mindset the importance of good health.

Dad also loved to eat and he ate like a marine. He was very partial to meat and ate limited selection of vegetables. He never followed the doctor's prescribed diet, but later in his life, he had to slow down his intake of rice and sweets because of his diabetes. He was religious, though, about taking his medications on time. With Mom's care, and maybe because of Dad's health regimen and the physical activity he got from his work per se, he was able to pull through with good health and able to work until that age.

Altogether, Dad worked for eighteen remarkable years in the U.S., having started in 1995. His fellow employees, from his first job to the last, were fond of him and would approach him to have a chat whenever they bumped into him in the supermarket or at church. In retirement, he spent all his time with Mom, looking after her.

When Dad retired, I suggested that he and Mom go on a cruise or overseas trip. I also told them they should go on vacation in the Philippines so they could reunite with their grandchildren and get to see their great-grandchildren. They were open to the idea but quite worried about Mom's health. They decided to give themselves a year to observe the changes in Mom's health before they plunged into a travel plan. Alas, Mom's health did not change for the better, and their travel plans were forgotten.

CHAPTER 12
MOM

When Chloe came to the U.S., she was involved with taking care of Dad and Mom. She rented a place of her own close by so she could come over to care for my parents every day after work. She provided geriatric care by assisting Mom with her personal hygiene, bathing, and changing of diapers and clothes. She also administered my parents' daily medications and doctor's appointments, ordered medications, shopped for the week's food supply, cooked, cleaned the apartment, and washed the laundry.

We all knew that Mom had a good appetite, so when the time came that she started eating very little or skipping meals, we knew something was wrong. She went through a malaise, had grown weaker and got exhausted easily. Her movements had become more sluggish and her reflexes were delayed or passive. She had her lethargic moments, preferring to lie in bed most of the time, not minding or caring to eat her meals or take her medicines. She stopped doing her regular activities, including her walking exercises. She seemed to have lost her zest for life. It gave us the red flag.

Doctors diagnosed Mom with congestive heart failure or CHF. My minimal understanding of CHF is that the heart is too weak to pump enough blood to the rest of the body.

After that, Mom had episodes of CHF that confined her to the hospital for as long as was needed.

Around February 2019, my *Tio* Francisco (*Tio* is the term for uncle in the Pangasinan vernacular), a doctor-brother of Dad, passed away. I attended the funeral in Los Angeles to represent my parents. It was difficult for my parents to travel because of Mom's declining health. That evening, Chloe called to say that Mom was in the hospital. I immediately flew back to Concord the next day.

At the John Muir Health, Concord Medical Center, my doctor-cousin visited Mom and briefly checked in on her. My cousin told us that Mom looked good, was alert, and carried on a good conversation with him. I took a leave from work so I could watch Mom at night while Dad and Chloe watched her during the day.

Mom's cardiologist, the good Dr. Kauffman, had passed away some years earlier. Dr. Graver took his place. He came one morning to do his round, assisted by a nurse. It was the first time I met him because it was Chloe who accompanied my parents to their doctor's appointments every time. I knew doctors to smile or say hello, just like all hospital personnel, when they entered the room to check on their patients. But this doctor was standoffish when he came in. He was detached from his patient. He was about six feet tall with bulging eyes and unkempt hair. I was told he was in his mid-sixties but he looked many years older than his age. I greeted Dr. Graver and the nurse as they walked in, just the same. He hurriedly went straight over to the computer to check Mom's records like he did not hear anything or there was nobody else in the room but him. The pretty nurse, however, courteously greeted me back and mom.

Dr. Graver, in his rumpled white coat, took a quick look

at Mom and blurted out like he was talking to himself, "There's no hope here. I think she's not going to last long."

I was stunned. I was wondering if I had heard him correctly or if I had taken his words out of context. Dr. Graver took another quick look at Mom and halfheartedly said, "Tsk, alright, get up and take a walk."

Mom tried to get up. I went over to assist her. She tried her best, but she really could not do it. She kindly asked Dr. Graver if she could do the walking the next day, thinking that if she was able to get some rest that day, she would have the energy to walk the next day. The intimidating doctor, with no remorse, said right to Mom's face, "Then this place is not for you. You can go home and wait."

I was wondering what he meant by, "You can go home and wait." Did he mean point-blank that all Mom needed to do was to just go home and wait to die? Why the hell did he even say that? Was he out of his mind or was he just indifferent? I think he was both.

Dr. Graver's faux pas disillusioned me. His language infuriated me. I could not stomach his rude and insensitive conduct. I censured him by saying, "This is my mother. She does not deserve this. Please get out."

Dr. Graver was nonchalant. He acted like he had not heard me. While he was still in the room, I tried my best to control my temper. I was reluctant to create a disturbance in the hospital. Besides, I did not want anything to add to our troubles while we were focusing our time and effort toward caring for Mom.

Dr. Graver quickly finished what he was doing. Without looking at us, he walked away while giving instructions to the nurse. Unfortunately, my mother had seen the lack of decency shamelessly displayed by her doctor. She whispered to me without contempt, "Frank, it is alright. The doctor said I did not have a chance. If that is the case, then just let me go."

My mother showed inner strength to be considerate enough and take the doctor's deplorable behavior in stride. She never showed dislike or said anything offensive against the doctor. I was not someone to judge or condemn the doctor, but he looked like he was impatient with his patients. The doctor seemed to have absolutely forgotten or abandoned the oath he took under medical and professional ethics. He seemed to have lost his set of values and doctor's mission to treat patients and save lives in the best possible and most caring way he could. His forte was to treat people with heart conditions. Maybe he should also consider curing his callous heart or simply have a "change of heart."

When Dad came, I did not tell him what happened because I did not want it to add to his worries. I did tell Chloe, who told me that the doctor had said something like that to Mom the last time they went for a checkup in his clinic some months back. I could not believe I met this doctor who acted like he was sentencing his patient, without tact and remorse.

The next day, Dr. Graver did not show up to do his rounds and a new cardiologist came in to check on Mom. The new doctor was courteous, attentive, and approachable. He helped facilitate Mom's transfer to a skilled nursing and rehabilitation center close by.

Dad, Chloe, and I kept the same schedule for watching Mom at the center. At night when I got sleepy, I curled up at the foot of Mom's bed. There was a space there where I could squeeze myself in because she had a small body frame. After two weeks, Mom suffered a mild heart attack. She was taken back to John Muir Health, Concord Medical

Center. This time she was brought straight to the intensive care unit.

The ICU rooms in the hospital were quite spacious. It accommodated one patient per room. We were allowed in as watchers. Mom was on oxygen support and standard IV medications, and her body was connected to all those tubes, apparatuses and monitoring devices. We constantly glanced at the monitors to check on any discrepancy. All I knew was if the layers of lines kept moving up and down, Mom's vital signs were stable.

Mom's vital signs were in good condition, but her health was actually deteriorating. She had difficulty articulating herself. She communicated through emaciated gestures like a very slight nod or pale smile.

The doctors talked to Chloe about the possibility of tube-feeding mom. Mom had not been getting the nutrients she needed and had developed ulcer because she had not been eating. She could not bite and swallow anymore. Tube-feeding could be done by two different methods. One involved inserting an orogastric tube into her throat and down into her stomach. The other one involved inserting a nasogastric tube into her nose and down into her throat. Mom knew how difficult and discomforting that would be for her to put up with, even if she was given anesthesia. Mom dreaded it either way.

As I looked at Mom, I would caress her hands. I longed to see the woman I knew who had been so captivating and beautiful in her youth. She had always been brimming with confidence and sweetness but enthralling with her humility and serenity. She had always been simple and unassuming. The long years that passed had yielded to many transformations. I looked at Mom once more in her sickbed. I saw

127

an eighty-eight-year-old woman whose arms were blackened and swollen from needle pricks. Her skin was creased and sagging, her hair had whitened and greyed, and her bones had gotten brittle over time. She was fragile and wasting away. My mother had been slackened by age and debilitated by ailment.

My mother never complained about her suffering as she carried on battling her ailments. She was dignified in her silence and accepted life's trials. I gently stroked her tousled hair, grateful for the long years she had devoted her life to her family. She was the woman who had cared for me from her womb to where I was now. She was a woman who had given her heart and soul to give me a good life. She was my mother who had given herself but wished for nothing in return.

When Dad was kissing Mom goodnight as he prepared to go home, Mom whispered to him not to leave her. As Mom wished, Dad did not go home that night. Since then, Dad stayed at the hospital every night. He would only go home to take a power nap and freshen up. He would then go back to the hospital as soon as he could to be at Mom's side. I would always see him gently holding her hands and praying for her recovery.

On March 29, 2019, Chloe brought Chinese food to the hospital for dinner, but we barely touched it. That night, Dad was listless and could not sleep. It was the same for me. At around 2:30 a.m., I got up from my chair and asked Dad if he wanted some coffee. I poured coffee from the thermos into paper cups. Since we felt pangs of hunger, I brought out some ham and cheese sandwiches. At a small corner table, we quietly ate an early breakfast.

I stood up to check on Mom. She looked okay but I

inadvertently heard her call out, "*Nanay*," (Mother). Mom was calling out to her mother. When Mom was at the skilled nursing and rehabilitation center, I had heard her say, "*Nay, hintayin niyo ako,*" (Mother, wait for me). Chloe also heard Mom calling out Nanay twice.

At first, I did not tell Dad about what we had heard Mom say because I did not want him to worry. There is a Filipino belief that when a person is dying, their departed loved ones will come to fetch them to accompany them to the afterlife. This time I decided to tell Dad so he would be prepared for whatever happened. Saddened by what I told him, Dad went over to Mom's side and stood there, holding her hands while he prayed.

A nurse came by to check on Mom. She seemed to be sound sleep. The nurse told us that Mom was doing well and persuaded us to get some rest so we would not get sick ourselves. I switched off the corner light and told Dad to go back to his chair to rest. At past 5 a.m., I got up from my chair. I thought the coldness and quietness in the room were disenchanting. The silence was so loud that it cast a pall over the room. As I stepped towards Mom's bed to check on her, I was wobbly from sleeplessness. At the flick of a finger, the deafening silence was busted by the horrifying beeping sound of the alarm coming from the heart monitor. Mom had gone into asystole (the cessation of electrical and mechanical activity of the heart, colloquially referred to as a flatline).

Right before my eyes, the heart monitor showed that the crooked line had bitterly changed into a straight line, the kind of thing I had only seen in movies. The monitor was connected to the nurse's station. Before I could call out to anyone, the nurses came rushing into the room. One of them went straight over and kneeled on the side of mom's bed and immediately initiated cardiopulmonary resuscitation (chest compression) on her.

Dad and I were dumbstruck. The turn of events had happened fast and we did not see it coming. One of the nurses politely led us outside to the waiting room to calm ourselves down as they struggled to revive Mom. I immediately called Chloe to tell her what was happening. I had not finished what I was telling her when I stopped and just broke down into tears.

Dad and I were sitting in the waiting room when two nurses came out of the ICU to talk to us. They told us that they had revived Mom which momentarily mitigated our anguish. Mom had no advance directive, so they asked me if I wanted her to be revived again in case another flatline happened.

"Please do everything you can to save my mother," I begged them.

In a few minutes, Chloe arrived in the waiting room. The three of us sat together on one small bench, stupefied, waiting for some news from the ICU. While I was hoping Mom would be fine, I was also trying to fight my apprehensions. At one point, I stood up to peer through the glass doors leading to the ICU hallway. I noticed a commotion in Mom's room. It was an unnerving moment and all I was able to do was go back to sit in the waiting room to pull myself together. We waited, and it was the longest wait ever with all the emotional pressure, tension and stress that built up.

This time, a middle-aged female doctor and a nurse came out from the ICU to see us. I stood up to greet them. The doctor took a deep breath and spoke gently. "For the second time, we had revived your mother." I heaved a sigh of relief.

The doctor continued. "She is stable right now. We are closely monitoring her. But we need to tell you that we will not do a revival procedure on her again. Your mother has gone through so much already. Her body has suffered enough."

Feeling down and discouraged, I was not able to answer the doctor immediately. In desperation, I soberly forced myself to reply. "Yes doc, I understand. Thank you for your help."

The doctor and I were standing in front of where Dad and Chloe were sitting. They could hear everything that the doctor and I talked about. I looked at Dad and Chloe's saddened faces. We all knew that this was one of the last straws for Mom. My vision was blurred by the tears in my eyes. Tears flowed freely on my face, purging me of my grief for a while. Dad and Chloe started to cry themselves. The reality of losing a loved one and the frustration of losing a battle to save a loved one gave me a heavy feeling. I felt a soft hand gently tapping on my left shoulder. It was the doctor comforting me. Before she headed back to the ICU, she said these words to me. "I know how it feels. Be strong."

After a few minutes, Mom experienced another flatline. A nurse called us back into the ICU so we would be by Mom's side as she took her last breath. We cried our hearts out as we expressed our love and said our final goodbyes. I said, "I love you Mom, and thank you." I was hoping that she could still hear me so she would know I had said those words to her. We video-called the family so they could see Mom and say their last words to her as we put our phones next to Mom's ears. Then we heard another alarm go off from one of the devices.

A nurse came over to my side and whispered, "She's

131

gone." I went over to Dad and whispered, "Dad, Mom is gone." Dad tearfully kissed Mom goodbye while he was holding her hand tightly.

It was past eight in the morning of March 30. I opened the window curtains that ushered in an awe-inspiring ray of sunshine in the room. It felt ethereal, as the new day with its gentle breeze and azure sky heralded my mother's journey into a pristine life in a verdant garden of peace and joy where there is an abundance of love and kindness in every corner.

My wife and son flew over in haste from the Philippines to attend Mom's funeral. Relatives and friends, including some of mom's former students came for the celebration of her life. Mom's students presented a video tribute which was shown during the wake. A representative from her students spoke during the eulogy. After Mom's funeral, one of her former students made another video tribute that we shared with family through social media platforms.

After Mom's demise, Dad pined for her all the time. He visited mom's niche at the Queen of Heaven Catholic Cemetery every day. Married to Mom for sixty-three years, it was painful for him to process the reality of living a life deprived of his one and only love. They had been inseparable, even unbreakable through the years. True love shaped their relationship and marriage and united them together till the end.

Being grief-stricken, Dad lost his appetite. He lost interest in his activities. He withdrew to his room most of the time. As he nursed his pain, he would become temperamental and irrational at times. He was healing the wounds from his loss when another loss cut deeper into his wound. Our oldest brother, *Kuya* Steve, died from a stroke in the Philippines at the age of sixty-two. When Chloe and I told him about it, he cried like a beaten man, defeated by losing two loved ones in five months. Chloe and I had to embrace him tightly to console him.

The sad news of my brother's passing brought my father into a state of denial. It was because the night before my brother died, Dad had just talked to him. Dad had told *Kuya* Steve to take care of his diabetes, blood pressure, and heart condition. My brother assured him that he did not need to worry because he was going to be okay. They had just had a warm conversation the night before he died. Dad could not believe that he had just talked to his son last night and he had been feeling good, and today his son was gone.

Everyone was stunned by my brother's death. The day before he died, his family was even celebrating their eldest daughter's birthday who worked in Saudi Arabia as a nurse. On that day, he was cheerful and high-spirited. Nobody expected his sudden demise.

When I was younger, I had conflicts with *Kuya* Steve because I was hardheaded. We had typical sibling misunderstandings, but many times, *Kuya* Steve would just forgive me and let me get away with it as his younger brother. We had parleyed and settled our differences a long time before I went to the U.S.

I had always given my love, respect, and admiration to my brother. He had always been a second father to me. I would always acknowledge his care and concern for his siblings. Because I got busy with my work in the U.S, I was only able to have occasional talks over the phone with him. I had been hoping to see him and *Kuya* James sometime in the future because we had not seen each other for a long time. It would be memorable if we could get together with Chloe who was already in the U.S. *Kuya* Steve left before we could even plan to see each other again. It reminded me that our time in this world is unpredictable and that our lives can change with the snap of a finger.

My father had intended to fly back home to the Philippines for my brother's burial, but his doctor advised him to forego his plan for health reasons. He felt so helpless because he was not able to send off his son, whom he had not seen for eighteen years since they had taken the Balikbayan trip in 2001.

The date for my brother's burial was September 12, 2019. It was September 11 in the U.S. September 10 happened to be Dad's birthday. On Dad's birthday, Chloe and I ordered food not to celebrate but to lift Dad's spirits up. We tried to cheer him up, but he was not up to it. We knew he was soothing his wounds. Chloe and I deeply and silently understood and felt what he deeply and silently felt. That day he did not care that it was his birthday. For him, there was nothing to celebrate because the next day was going to be his son's burial. We watched my brother's wake and funeral services through live streaming, but Dad would avoid watching it. My father had the loneliest birthday he had ever had in his whole life.

CHAPTER 13
DAD

After some time had passed, I could see that Dad was trying his best to move on as he struggled to overcome his grief and loneliness. Still, the effects of his grief took a toll on his health. His pleasure for eating had not been the same. He ceased doing his routine activities like walking, exercising, and watering the plants. He lost weight and had grown weak.

When my sister and I started going back to work, he was left alone in the apartment the whole day, every day, adding to his loneliness. During the pandemic, he was domesticated the whole time and led a more solitary and sedentary life. He fell on the floor three times, even though he walked carefully.

As much as we tried our best to keep safe during the Covid-19 pandemic, our efforts were not enough to fend off infection. Dad was very careful and followed all the health protocols even though he was at home all the time. He wore masks and gloves, washed his hands frequently, practiced social distancing, even with us at home, and avoided going out of the apartment.

During the first week of December 2020, Dad tested positive for Covid. We were unaware of his infection because he never showed any symptoms. We only got to know about Dad's infection after he was taken to the hospital when

Chloe called 911.

It was early evening when Chloe entered Dad's apartment after work. She sensed that something was wrong. The lights were not on even though it was already dark. She found Dad still lying in bed, like he was into one of those normal instances when he was just lazy to get up and oblivious of the time. He was not feverish, delirious, or gasping for breath. Chloe could talk to him normally but he would give confused answers or was oblivious of what he was saying or doing. His bed was soaked with pee. His phone rang and he would not answer it, which was unlikely of him to do. His cell phone was right next to him on the bed. Chloe asked Dad to get up so she can help him change his clothes, but he seemed heedless to get up or change his wet diaper and pajamas.

When he got up from bed, Chloe assisted him to go to the bathroom, which was just a few steps from his bed. While they were slowly walking, he fell on the floor. Chloe tried to lift him up but he was too heavy for her. She tried asking Dad to lift himself up so she could assist him but he could not move his body even a bit. My sister was stunned because my father had never been like that before. She called 911. Dad was taken to the emergency room of the John Muir Health, Concord Medical Center.

Earlier in March of that same year, Dad was hospitalized in the same hospital in Concord for mild stroke. He woke me up at 7 a.m., gasping for breath. When I called 911, paramedics at first thought it was a case of Covid-19. At that time, Covid-19 cases were starting to surge at an alarming rate in most parts of the country. On that day, I was told that I could not stay in the hospital as a watcher. Nobody was even allowed to stay in the hospital lobby. I saw medical workers and hospital staff in groups being briefed by their respective supervisors. I presumed they were executing immediate and serious precautionary measures and preparations to implement Covid-19 health protocols. After a few days of confinement, Dad was released from the hospital. After two days, President Trump announced a lockdown in the country with a mandate to follow health protocols like wearing a mask and social distancing.

That December day when Chloe called me at work to inform me that Dad was taken to the hospital, I immediately asked for some time off and rushed to get there. I met Chloe in her car in the parking area because we were not allowed inside the hospital. We called Dad's doctor who informed us that Dad had tested positive for Covid-19 and would be moved to the John Muir Medical Center in Walnut Creek for confinement.

Subsequently, that night, I developed sore throat and fever with a temperature of 103 degrees Fahrenheit. I quarantined myself at home. The next day, Chloe went for a Covid test and was found to be positive. Since she was a government employee, she asked to facilitate her quarantine at a government-sponsored quarantine hotel in Oakland.

Since we were not allowed to visit Dad, we talked to him over the phone all the time. For his first two days in the hospital, he was feeling good. He told me that he just finished the walking exercise the nurse had asked him to do. He said he had tucked away a good lunch and did not feel any manifestation of the ailment. He was more concerned about us being infected. We never told him that we were infected with Covid ourselves to spare him from worrying. We told him to concentrate on getting well and not worry about us because we are doing okay.

For seven days, I battled the symptoms of Covid-19 at home. I experienced chills, chest pain, dry cough, sore throat, diarrhea, vomiting, and persistent high fever. On the seventh day, I had difficulty breathing. I brought myself to the hospital close by our apartment. They found me positive with Covid-19 and was immediately transported to the John Muir Medical Center in Walnut Creek for confinement, the same hospital where Dad was confined. It was also the same hospital where Dad worked for many years.

By that time, Dad's condition had become aggravated. He was moved to the ICU. He had grown weak and spoke inaudibly with much effort. The three of us were confined but we never told him about it. Dad never knew our proximity in the same hospital.

During the time we were hospitalized, Covid cases were widespread, and all hospitals were brimming with patients. Tracking down the origin of our infection was quite hard. During the pandemic, Dad never went out of his apartment except once to pay rent when he forgot to give the check to Chloe. The rental office was a few steps away and it was never crowded. It took less than five minutes to go to the rental office to pay the rent and be back home. Despite the fact that Dad always wore mask and gloves, washed his hands, practiced social distancing, and stayed in a safe environment, it still was not enough to deter infection. The virus could infect us anywhere at any time. We are all vulnerable because the virus is not visible.

The virus could have been transmitted through me since I commuted on public transportation and my work required me to interact with customers. It could also have been Chloe who worked from home at the start of the pandemic but regularly went to stores and restaurants for our food. The two of us were the ones exposed to the elements. It was a relief that Chloe endured only mild symptoms. She never felt anything more than losing her sense of taste and smell. It was Dad and I who got it the worst.

I stayed in the hospital for six days. I developed pneumonia from my Covid infection. I was alone in my hospital room as there were no visitors or watchers allowed to enter the hospital. Nurses and doctors would come every four hours to check on my condition and administer medications like Remdesivir and Decadron. They did numerous laboratory examinations and bloodwork on me.

In my hospital room, I prayed the Rosary every day for the recovery of the three of us. I wanted to get well fast but as I battle Covid-19 and pneumonia, I pondered if I was going to get well or not, or live or not. Tagging along were my concerns about my family, money to send home, my job, my dreams, and just about everything else. My mind was willing to move on, but my body was helpless and powerless. Even if I wanted to move, I could not lift a finger to do anything at all. I had started to have a feeling of ennui while in my sickbed.

Then one day while I was saying my prayers, something happened spontaneously that turned my life around—I surrendered myself to the Lord God. Amidst the tranquility embracing my whole being, I whispered to Him, "Lord, it's in your hands." Shortly after that, I felt like everything stopped. I felt like I was at zero and empty. I felt like a blank piece of paper.

I suddenly felt relieved from the questions and worries that bothered me. I stopped being restless and impatient. I stopped worrying about my condition. I lost my stubbornness and pride. I felt I had no control of what was happening.

I let it be and went with the flow. It was like if I live or die, so be it. I was surprisingly calm. If the Lord God was in control, why should I be afraid? What power or right did I have to stop or change or question God's plan?

I tried to discern the meaning of what I felt. My comprehension was not about theoretical or philosophical connotations. I internalized it as more spiritual than anything else. Maybe I simply had gone through a deep reflection or meditation or soul-searching. Or maybe I just carried out a heartfelt prayer or deep heart-to-heart talk with the Lord.

After that, I started to feel better. I felt that I was destined to get well from Covid-19 for a new purpose in life. I felt I was blessed to be given a fresh start to a new chapter in my life with a mandate to start with a clean slate. I took it as a second chance at life. It was a defining moment.

When I had completely recovered, my encounter with Covid-19 impacted on my subconscious mind. I thought about it as a lesson in life, a humbling experience as well as a turning point in my life. It was like losing everything and starting again from nothing. It was a new beginning as I received new blessings and opportunities while I struggle to rise above challenges and obstacles. It had given me the courage and dignity to work on what I needed to change. I learned to appreciate the gifts that I receive every day and reset my priorities in life. I opened my eyes to the truth about life which led me to value life even more.

To launch my new life, I was emboldened to ask forgiveness from people I had wronged which included my wife and son. Asking for forgiveness from people mitigated the burden in my heart as it was a humble acceptance of my mistakes, even if I knew that some of those people I asked forgiveness from had also done me wrong. One by one, things fell into place. It was hard to start again, but there was a feeling of lightness because I had never realized that while I was healing from Covid-19, I was also trekking on the path to heal my life and soul.

As I recovered in my hospital bed, Dad's condition took a serious turn. It devastated us that we could not even reach out to him. Suddenly, he could not talk anymore. We contented ourselves with one-way communication. If we called Dad, the nurse would answer his cell phone and turn the speaker on. The nurse would place the cellphone close to Dad's ear so we could then deliver our monologues. As soon as we were done, the nurse would turn off the phone.

Dad was under constant monitoring because his heartbeat would slow down and his blood pressure, oxygen levels and blood sugar levels would drop. He was alternately put on oxygen, then BiPap, then oxygen and then BiPap again. Then he was placed on a ventilator. When his ventilator did not work, they did an intubation procedure. Chloe received daily updates on Dad's condition from the nurses.

I was discharged from the hospital while Chloe finished her two-week quarantine. It was December 20, 2020, five days before Christmas. I lost a notable amount of weight, but I was glad to be home and well. At home, I continued to worry about Dad. I prayed for a miracle, hoping against hope, to see Dad back to his bubbly self again.

In the early evening of December 22nd, a nurse called my sister to tell her Dad was in critical condition. They asked her if she could come to the hospital right away. I wanted to go with Chloe, but I was still weak and easily got tired. If I tried to walk just a few steps, I would gasp for air. Besides, I was still required to be quarantined for two weeks after my hospital discharge.

Chloe was allowed to take a quick look at Dad through the glass partition at the ICU. A doctor talked to her about the medical team's fears about Dad's chance of survival. His life was hanging on by a thread on life support. She saw Dad looking emaciated as he was lying face down on the bed while the nurses attended to him. The nurses explained to her that having Dad lying face down would help him to breathe better. She could only embrace and kiss Dad through the glass panel that separated them.

Chloe hosted a Zoom call to enable the family to say their parting words. In this virtual platform, the family tearfully sent their love and farewells to Dad. I asked for Dad's forgiveness and said I loved him. Despite that, I never said goodbye to him. I still held on to my belief that he would get well. Up to the last minute, I was still hoping for a miracle, even though I knew he was struggling for his life. It was not over until it was over. It was past 7 p.m. when Chloe called. She told me Dad was gone. In front of the bedroom altar at home, I offered my prayers and said, "If it's your will, I accept it."

The radio in the living room was on. It played one of our favorite Christmas songs with its heartwarming melody. "Have yourself a merry little Christmas, let your heart be light . . ." I walked into the living room and sat down on the sofa. The Christmas carol continued. "Through the years, we'll always be together, if the Fates allow. Hang a shining star upon the highest bough . . ." In my mind I told him, "Merry Christmas, Dad."

As I listened to the song, I asked myself how could I have a merry Christmas when my father had just died. I looked around the apartment. It was now empty of life. It was as gloomy and cold as the winter night. Alone, I cried, carrying the pain in silence, and filling the room with sadness.

I looked around the living room. There was no Christmas tree, no gifts, no twinkling lights. I looked outside and there was no *parol* hanging on the porch. There was no more Dad and Mom living in the apartment. I was looking for them to fill the apartment with their laughter and good-natured banters. I was wondering where our home had gone. I felt the emptiness because they were the very people who had transformed the apartment into a home for me. They were the very people who gave me a home in America. They were the very people who gave me the warmth and solace of a home away from my home with my family in the Philippines.

The radio played another Christmas song. "I'll be home for Christmas. You can plan on me. Please have snow and mistletoe, and presents by the tree . . ." There was something in the song that rippled with the classic relevance of Christmas to everyone, whether you are rich or poor, alone or with family, happy or sad. It re-echoed the epiphany of the Christmas spirit. The greatest gift that we can ever receive on Christmas is the warmth of home and love from family.

The song continued to play on the radio. "Christmas Eve will find me, where the love light gleams. I'll be home for Christmas, if only in my dreams . . ." When the song ended, I gave thanks to the Lord for the blessing of having had many years experiencing Christmas with family at home. I was thinking that perhaps Dad and Mom had a home someplace where they have the greatest and happiest Christmas celebrations of all time. I wiped my tears dry and savored the memories of the Yuletide season that my whole family used to enjoy together.

During Christmas time in the Philippines, my family had

always made it a point to come home and celebrate together. When my parents migrated to the U.S. and some of the grandkids worked overseas, we still connected and celebrated together through virtual platforms. Now that Dad and Mom were gone, my family continued to connect with each other as we strive to make our family whole and piece together our lives with the love and memories my parents left us.

As I continued to live my life, I learned to come to terms with my loss and grief. I intertwined it with the meaning and value of life. I took steps to move on and seek my purpose in life. I looked back at memories of Christmases past. It brought smiles and laughter. It also brought regrets and sadness, realizing it was in the past. I resolved to go on with my life even if I no longer had Dad and Mom by my side. I would go on with my life with their memories in my heart.

The holiday season was a significant part of our family togetherness. It was sad that the timing of Dad's passing was during that time. Despite what happened, I told Chloe that we would carry on our Christmas celebrations. On Christmas Eve, I told her to order food for *Noche Buena*. To supplement what she ordered, I cautiously sorted through and picked out various food that was in the freezer. Even though I was still weak, I took time out to patiently fry some chicken drumsticks and grilled leftover Black Angus steak. We had a scrumptious Christmas Eve dinner.

Chloe had made a last-minute effort to buy me a gift which she gave after dinner. We were silent and sad, but we tried our best not to show it. We knew it would never be the same again, but we also knew that what we were doing was what Dad and Mom would have wanted us to do. My parents were there in spirit with us. We had the foundation of family and home inside of us to help us move on and live our lives. Chloe and I did the same thing when we welcomed in the New Year with a celebration that we used to do with the whole family.

I recalled that morning when I had bade goodbye to Dad as I hurried to leave for work. That was the last time I saw him. That afternoon, he was taken by paramedics to the hospital. I never saw him again, not even in the hospital where we were both confined and not even at his cremation. He was just gone, like he had vanished into thin air. Like a thief in the night, the Covid-19 virus took a healthy and loving eighty-seven-year-old father and grandfather away and he was gone forever.

I did not have even one iota of chance to get closure with Dad. The only time I got to hold Dad again was when I picked up the urn that contained his ashes. That was the last time I held him. Still, I was not able to say goodbye to him. Maybe his sudden demise had not sunk in yet. The hardest goodbye is the one left unsaid. At the time of Dad's funeral, Covid cases were continuously spiking. We had to follow health protocols. Public gatherings were restricted. At Dad's burial, it was only me, Chloe, our two aunts, and a cousin in attendance. We got some solace by thinking that Dad must be happy now, together with Mom, in a world far better than ours.

The scourge of Covid-19 virus caused many members of our family to suffer from the infection. It painfully tore my family apart when it took my father's life. Four months later, it took *Kuya* James's life in the Philippines. He was only in his fifties and left a young family.

The events in my life left an indelible mark on my consciousness. When Dad, Chloe, and I were infected by Covid-

19, it was *Kuya* James who was in the Philippines, who was the most worried. He would call every day to check on us. He did not have the slightest idea that he and other members of our family would get infected themselves. He never knew that he would die from it and be a tragic addition to the statistics of a continuously growing number of Covid deaths.

I remember *Kuya* James as the one who provided comical relief to the family with his funny antics and jokes. He was the most understanding and forgiving person I had ever known. When we were kids, we got into several fistfights over petty things that are normal kid stuff, but we never got into a serious sibling rivalry. He would always forgive me as his younger brother, even if it was my fault. We would easily forget our quarrels. We became buddies instead of foes.

The pandemic caused misery to many people throughout the world. It mercilessly took many lives since the time it started. My family and I had been struck hard by it. Looking back, although the pandemic caused agony to me and my family, it became a way that brought me closer to God.

One time as I prayed before the suffering Christ on the cross, I was enlightened about why I had to bear the cross of losing my family one by one. I thought that God will not give me trials without a reason. He knows what and how much load to give me. He knows which door to open next when He closed a door on me. He would open not just a door but a portal for me.

For all we know, at the end of the day, trials are hidden blessings. An avenue to find success and fulfillment. A chance to learn from our mistakes and change for the better. Trials and suffering brings out the best in us and enable us to see who we really are and what we can do in life. I thought that if God gave me a burden, I must be valuable to Him because I have a mission and He is shaping me into the very best version of myself that I can ever imagine to be. We all have a purpose in life. For everything that we go through, there is a greater truth and beauty and the reason behind it. God Himself let Jesus suffer and die on the cross to save us from our sins. "For God so loved the world, that He gave His only son, so that everyone who believes in Him will not perish but have eternal life." God has all the answers we are seeking. I put my trust and belief in Him.

In a span of two years, my family went through tragic losses that scarred our lives. My parents and two brothers died at different intervals from different illnesses. The successive deaths in the family were the nightmares of my life. They were nightmares that I could not wake myself up from to shake them off. My nightmares were agonizingly real. The saddest moments of my life were when I had to say goodbye to my loved ones, one after the other. I have no answers as to why all these happened in my life, but it opened my eyes to the gift of accepting and understanding, to discover my purpose and see the meaning of life, to embrace the lessons that I learned and to value my life and the life of others.

When I lost my parents and brothers, it reminded me that there is no permanency in this life. It is only in the afterlife that we can find infinity. Each life has a story that ends. Each life is a journey with a destination. For some, the journey was the destination itself. Perhaps it was how we lived our lives and how we loved and treated each other that defines our destination. Perhaps it was how we accomplished our mission that completes our journey or makes our destination.

Since our stories all have endings and our journeys have destinations, our lives have their own timeframes. When my mother was in the ICU and her heart monitor displayed a flatline and set off the alarm, it reminded me that life is transitory. When your time is up, it is what it is. Nobody has the power to hold onto or extend it.

Sometimes we forget about the brevity of human life. Sometimes we act like we are immortal when we get everything we wanted in life. Being reminded of our brief time in this world gives us the chance to make the most of our time and not waste it. It gives us the conviction about what to value in life. It gives us a better understanding and outlook on life. It motivates us to show our love to our loved ones whenever we can while we are still beside them.

Life is fleeting. Even though I lived with my parents for almost eighteen years in the U.S., it seemed like those long years were short-lived. How I wish I had given the best of myself to them when they were still alive. It was not that I did not love and care for them when they were living, but I felt that what I gave them was not good enough. I could have done better. I thought that if I were able to give my all when they were still living, there would be no regrets and it would not matter anymore whether I lived with them for a short time or longer. I tried to comfort myself that I tried my best even if I fell short. It reminded me of the importance of the present that whatever you can do or give in the present, do it and give it now. We cannot bring back the past and we never know what lies ahead of us.

I realize I could have steered clear of hurting my parent's feelings if I had been more understanding and obedient to them. I could have strengthened our relationship if I had cared for them with more compassion and patience. I could have attained a more meaningful relationship with them if I had given more of my time and love to them. I should have done all those things when I had all those chances during the years that I stayed with them.

I knew that when my parents were turning old and gray, they longed for a home with the warmth, love, and care of their children and grandchildren. Since I lived with them, they were hoping to realize that at least partly, with me. I was the physical presence and family representative for them who somehow covered for the absence of my siblings. I understood that as the years went by, my parents had borne the pain of having to break away from the close-knit family ties they had when they moved to the U.S. It was unfortunate that my work and dreams took a lion's share of the time that I was supposed to spend with them. I knew my parents would have understood my absences and situation, but I deeply regret my shortcomings. I had lost the time to be with them. My opportunity had passed. I could not make up for it. All I could do now was to look back with regret.

When Chloe came to the U.S., she was able to spare more time and give more care to my parents than I ever did in the short time that she had the chance to be with them. I saw how much Dad and Mom appreciated Chloe's hands-on efforts to care for them. My parents also appreciated my efforts, but I was not really good at providing hands-on patient care. Despite my shortcomings, I hope I was still able to give them the love and care they deserved, even in part. My experience made me understand better the essence of family that my parents valued so much. It gave me the ultimate feeling of connection and being a part of each other in the family.

When Dad and Mom passed, that was when I realized how significant their longing was to keep a home filled with love and care. For them, home was family. Home was love and care. Home was happiness and shelter. Home was what you felt when you were inside your house. Home is where you learned that it was the value of your family and life that was important, not the value of your house.

As my parents grew older and sickly, they continued to carry in their hearts the life and home they wanted to have. At the sunset of their lives, they wanted a home, not a house. They wanted a life, not an existence. They wanted to see the family together. They wanted to bond with their children. They wanted a home that they could feel in their hearts. They wanted to have the home that they knew, together with their children, back in their hearts.

I pray that everyone will have a home where the whole family can live together. A home where everything is true and good, simple and free, warm and stable. A home that builds oneness and harmony. A home that builds memories that last. A home that builds a strong foundation of love and respect.

My Dad and Mom have gone home. They have gone to an eternal home of overflowing peace and joy. They were laid to rest in a niche at Queen of Heaven Catholic Cemetery in Pleasant Hill, beside the niche of Mom's sister and mother. We committed Dad and Mom's ashes in one niche, as they had wished. Until the very end, my parents chose to stay together. Chloe and I visit them regularly on a weekly basis. My parents are gone, but they will never be forgotten.

EPILOGUE

September 10, 2021, was Dad's first birthday after his death. On that day, I made sure I cooked spaghetti. The reason was the year before, I had promised Dad that I would cook spaghetti for him, but I never got to do it. I promised him again on Thanksgiving, but I failed to make it for the second time. December came and I told him I would cook it for him on Christmas. He died three days before Christmas.

A few months before his death, he also asked me to fix the stereo so he could listen to his favorite CDs. I said yes, but I never got the chance to fix it. I have now fixed the stereo for him, even though he is not there anymore to play his CDs.

I missed Mom asking me if I want breakfast. Since I was always in a hurry, I would respond with, "No Mom, but thanks." Still, Mom would cook my favorites—bacon, scrambled eggs, toasted bread, and hot chocolate, in case I changed my mind. Mom was right. There were times I got tempted to take a quick bite before I left for work.

When my parents died, I tried my best to do some little things that would continue to honor them. In the new restaurant I was working at, I bought bunches of roses and gave it to mothers among our customers and coworkers on Mother's Day. On Father's Day, I bought pizza for my coworkers. I was doing those things in honor of my parents. There are many ways to remember our parents and we can do it on any day, whether it is a special day, or just an ordinary day. A simple prayer is a great way to honor them.

I grieved when I lost my parents. Their death was a sad ending, but it gave me a new beginning and a new outlook on life. Their death sadly closed doors but it opened other doors for me to continue my journey in life. Their death was a loss, but it gave me the strength to find my way down the dark and winding road. My parents' passing was a lonely farewell, but I knew they would be happy to see me move on to face the challenges and grab the rewards that lay ahead. Their death was not an end to our ties. It had just been taken a notch higher. It gave me realizations, discoveries, and a better understanding about the meaning of life and family.

The Fourth Commandment clearly states, "Honor Thy Father and Thy Mother." Children have a moral obligation to love and care for their parents. Our parents should have their place on a pedestal. If we can idolize famous people for their work and achievements, we should memorialize our parents in our hearts for their love and sacrifices. Parents are unsung heroes. Whoever we are now, whatever we have become and whatever we have achieved in life, our parents have made a big contribution. We owe it to them.

Living with my parents in the U.S. gave me a goldmine of insightful experiences. It was different from my experience of home in the Philippines because I was young then, having a fun and easy life and without a care in the world.

My life with them in the U.S. was meaningful to me because I lived with them for many years, just the three of us, together in a foreign land. We only had each other for support, and together we faced the odds, hardships, struggles, and loneliness of uprooted and replanted individuals.

It tested the ties that bound us as parents and son. It helped that I lived with them in the U.S. when I was already a mature family man. It would have been different if I had lived with them when I was still young and single. Because of that, I was able to have a good grownup perspective about them that taught me valuable lessons and made me a better person.

When I was young, I knew my parents loved me, but I failed to seriously appreciate them and reciprocate. I even misunderstood my parents' good intentions and decisions in life. I knew the importance of family but failed to see how deep-rooted it could be. During my adolescent years, I had other priorities that I cared more about than family matters.

I also had misconceptions and skepticism about my parents when I was young. I had expectations and standards that I was hoping they could meet. I compared them to other parents I knew who were more accomplished. I thought I knew better than my parents. I thought they had failed in some ways.

When I stayed in America with them, I discovered I had been wrong the whole time. I was a failure in many ways, not them. I had confused my mind with mistaken notions of what a good parent should be in terms of what I saw in other parents. I was blind not to see them just as they were, selfless. It was their selflessness that I received. They gave their whole selves, their lives, and their hearts to me and our whole family.

My parents never sized me up by the way I looked and carried myself. They never compared my achievements and material gains with other children they knew. Instead, they looked at my character, thoughts, and feelings. They looked at me for who I was, from the inside. I learned to look at my parents the same way. When I did that, I saw their true worth, right to the core. I found a parental love that was true, whole, and unpretentious. It was parental love that was not half-baked and sugarcoated because it was pure and honest.

Living with my parents was a discovery of their deepest love that redefined how I looked at them and at life itself. It redefined what they were to me as their son, and what I had become because of them. Living with them made me see their deepest thoughts and emotions. Despite our generational gap, they would always understand and make efforts to bridge that gap. There were times when I thought that what they were doing was not good for me. But at the end of the day, I would learn that what they were doing was for my own good after all. Parents will do anything for their children's sake We are always confident and secure with our parents' love and affection.

My parents may not have been perfect, but no one is. They made their own mistakes and had failures as I did. Their efforts to make up for or correct those imperfections for their family inspired me to rectify my own wrongs and failures too.

My parents' pieces of advice and words of wisdom, whether they were clichés or not, were a treasure chest of life lessons and inspirations. I have resolved to keep their advice and those words of wisdom to lift my spirit and to beam them out as my guiding light whenever I stray from my path. I consider them to be some of my parents' legacies that I will pass on to my son for his own journey.

It is true that everyone's parents are their one and only. We cannot change them or replace them. Nobody can really substitute for them. Parents are God's gift to us as we are

God's gift to our parents. My parents were a strong foundation, an integral component, a uniting force, and an inspiration to our family. They were our fortress and shield from the chaotic and turbulent world we live in. They were our sanctuary that brought peace to our weary and battled souls. Their love epitomized the pulchritude of true parental love.

I got to witness firsthand Dad and Mom's travails and triumphs, their sorrows and joys, and their never-ending efforts to keep the family whole and connected despite being separated across the ocean. I got to witness their profound faith in God that inspired me to have a strong and deep faith myself.

I want to thank you, Daddy and Mommy, for the journey with you. I was blessed to have you as parents who enriched my life with your love and care. My journey with you fortified my personal struggles and influenced the path to my destiny. My journey with you in the U.S. was a blessing. As I continue with my journey, I want to thank you for being a big part of it. And even though you are gone, I know you will still be there with me on my journey, every step of the way.

Thank you for being magnanimous to the family, even if we had nothing to give back. Thank you for thriving on what you could give to us instead of what we could give to you. Thank you for being unconditional in your sacrifices, patience, and understanding. Thank you for the gift of parenthood that you gave us. Thank you for guiding and protecting us without grandstanding it.

Dad and Mom, thank you for accepting my flaws and shortcomings while never failing to correct me for my wrongdoings. Thank you for putting up with my stubbornness while you presented what was right and wrong.

Thank you for being selfless and forgiving as you filled me with your words of affirmation and encouragement. Thank you for trusting me and believing in me when nobody else did.

Dad and Mom, you never turned your back on me, even if you could have. You never gave up on me, even if you had all the reasons to do so. Through all the vicissitudes, you remained steadfast in your unfathomable love and guidance. Your unequivocal support kept me buoyant amidst the rough seas. You never made me feel like I was a failure or loser when I lost the race. I was never alone and forsaken when everyone else had gone away. You will have a special place in my heart forever. I can never thank you enough.

Dad and Mom, I am sorry for my faults that caused you trouble and misery. I am sorry for answering back, that hurt and broke your hearts. I am sorry for being indifferent, disobedient, and irresponsible, that intimidated you. I know there is no rewind in our lives to bring back the past and make amends. But I will continue to be the best son that I can be for you, even now that you are both gone. I would not trade the life I had with you for anything else in this world, even though all that is left of that now is memories.

Wherever you are, Daddy and Mommy, I pray that the Lord will always embrace you with His divine love. My gratitude for you is beyond words for touching and changing my life. When you passed away, your love did not die with you. Your love lives on and continues to heal my heart. It is as ageless as the memories you left behind.

I will never tire of saying, "I Love You, Dad and Mom," like you never tired of loving me. I have no qualms about saying those words even a thousand times. It is about gratitude and giving back. It is about showing my love and reverence to you. That is the only way I can pay a small tribute to you, even if you are both gone and far away now. For when you were alive, I regret that I never got a chance to say those simple but profound words to the both of you. I regret it is too late.

Now I know that every moment matters, that every word is precious, and that every show of love and kindness is priceless. But no matter how late it is, I will always express how much I love you both because that means your love still lives in my heart. I will carry your love with me wherever my journey brings me. I missed the home you provided for me in America. I missed the comfort of home after a long day and the smell of hot meals from the kitchen. I missed the laughter, the music, the stories, the jokes, and the happiness that filled our home. Most of all, I missed the care and concern, and the warmth of your love and affection that fully enveloped my being. I get comfort believing that you now live in a perfect home of eternal bliss and peace, together.

Daddy and Mommy, thank you and I love you.

Every praise is to our God.

ABOOKS

ALIVE Book Publishing
is an imprint of Advanced Publishing LLC,
3200 A Danville Blvd., Suite 204, Alamo, California 94507

Telephone: 925.837.7303
alivebookpublishing.com

www.ingramcontent.com/pod-product-compliance
Lightning Source LLC
Chambersburg PA
CBHW021334090426
42742CB00008B/606